D1559304

Just
Like Us

Just
Like Us

15 Biblical Stories with
Take-Away Messages
You Can Use in Your Life

Frank Minirth, M.D.
Don Hawkins, D.Min.
Roy Vogel, Ph.D.

[handwritten inscription: To Melissa / Bland Co - labor in LP / at SEBC endeavors, and / and student of His Word! / Isaiah 40:31]

JOSSEY-BASS
A Wiley Imprint
www.iossevbass.com

Published by Jossey-Bass
A Wiley Imprint
989 Market Street, San Francisco, CA 94103-1741   www.josseybass.com

Permissions continued on p. 224.

Jossey-Bass books and products are available through most bookstores. To contact Jossey-Bass
directly call our Customer Care Department within the U.S. at 800-956-7739, outside the
U.S. at 317-572-3986, or fax 317-572-4002.

Jossey-Bass also publishes its books in a variety of electronic formats. Some content that
appears in print may not be available in electronic books.

Library of Congress Cataloging-in-Publication Data

Minirth, Frank.
    Just like us : 15 biblical stories with take-away messages you
can use in your life / Frank Minirth, Don Hawkins, Roy Vogel
      p. cm.
    Includes bibliographical references.
    ISBN 0-7879-6904-4 (alk. paper)
    1. Bible stories, English.   I. Hawkins, Don.   II. Vogel, Roy, date.   III. Title.
BS550.3.M56 2004
220.9'505—dc22   2003026846

Printed in the United States of America
FIRST EDITION
HB Printing   10 9 8 7 6 5 4 3 2 1

Contents

Preface   ix

Acknowledgments   xv

1. Gideon: An Ordinary Man with an Extraordinary Purpose   1
2. Job: Reacting to Multiple Trials   13
3. Moses: A Man of Ups and Downs   23
4. Caleb: How to Finish Well   41
5. Naomi: Battling Adversity and Bitterness   55
6. David: Defeating Life's Giants   71
7. Solomon: A Wise Man with an Achilles' Heel   87
8. Elijah: Committed but Not Perfect   101
9. Hezekiah: In Pursuit of God   111
10. Jeremiah: A Man of Many Contrasts   119
11. Daniel: A Mentally Healthy Man   133
12. John the Baptist: A Man Out of Step with Society   149
13. Martha: Focused on Performance   157
14. Peter: The Risk Taker   173
15. Paul: Insane, Obsessive, or Genius?   189

Conclusion   213

Notes   215

The Authors   221

To our grandchildren:
Hannah Fox, Chris Varela, Albert Varela,
Holly Hancock, Mary Hancock, Brandon Hancock,
Makenzie Hancock, Karissa Justice,
Hannah Justice, Rebekah Justice, Josiah Justice,
Micah Justice, and Ariana Lee Teel

Preface

Were people in the Bible really like you and me? We may wonder if it's even possible when we read about individuals such as Paul, Peter, Martha, David, and Elijah; they seem ten feet tall, spiritually speaking. We assume they didn't have major problems, or we think that the strength they had for overcoming life's trials was far beyond what is available to us today. Yet an examination of these individuals' lives reveals a different story. Every giant of biblical days had an Achilles' heel, just like us.

Although the biblical accounts of these individuals were divinely inspired, they themselves were mere mortals, with the same strengths, weaknesses, and struggles we face today. We can identify with these people and learn lessons from their lives that will enable us to cope with the stresses of the twenty-first century. From these people who lived and worshiped God thousands of years ago, we can learn how to be spiritually and mentally healthy today.

The societies in which these biblical characters lived were vastly different from ours—no telephones, no watches, and no freeways. Their world was not as scientific as ours. They did not face the threat of nuclear warfare. But the threats they faced were as real to them as the ones we face are to us. They grappled with the same life-and-death issues as we do. They were just like us, and their lives left us take-away messages from the past that can affect our choices today.

For example, Gideon was an ordinary man who was fearful at the thought of an extraordinary challenge. We have each felt that way at times. Indeed, if most Christians were asked if they feel fearful at times, or just feel ordinary, most would say they do. Roadblocks to the tasks facing us may seem insurmountable. And yet we, like Gideon, are asked to take on formidable missions. How can we answer such a daunting call? This book offers forthright take-away messages to empower you to move from living the ordinary to accomplishing the extraordinary.

Frequently the ups and downs of life today are so intense as to produce psychological trauma. "The puzzling, and disturbing effects of psychological trauma on human functioning have been described for generations, going as far back as Homer's *Iliad*," stated the German doctor Rafael Ornstein.[1] Who today has not experienced the trauma of having "up" times, only to be followed by times of feeling low? Almost daily in our roles as psychiatrist, minister and college president, and psychologist, we encounter once-vibrant Christians who now feel discouraged. We, like Moses, may be up at one time only to fall down when adversity hits. Moses' story teaches us how to live through life's traumatic emotional roller-coaster. Regardless of unfruitful past choices, we can make new wholesome choices today. Moses can teach us.

Furthermore, we all want to finish life on earth well. How can we do that? Brad Reddick and Ned Cassem have aptly stated, "Through the advancement of medical technology and practice the human lifespan has grown. This has created fertile ground for opportunities and for conflict."[2] Indeed, this is true; yet even in our contemporary society, we can take away relevant precepts from the times of Caleb to help us live our lives more fully.

And who has not felt angry at times? The words in the English language dealing with anger are legion. Nouns for anger include *rage*, *resentment*, *annoyance*, and *fury*. Verbs for anger include *infuriate*, *annoy*, *displease*, *exasperate*, and *provoke*. Related words—*irate*, *irk*, *irascible*, *pique*, and *bitterness*—are myriad. And who hasn't become familiar with phrases such as *road rage* and *going postal*? Obviously, anger is an enormous problem, one we all share. When the issue of anger is addressed on our radio program "Life Perspectives" or at workshops offered through the Minirth Clinics, the response indicates an overwhelming number of people seeking answers to this problem. How do we battle adversity and the resulting bitterness? Perhaps the life of Naomi offers take-away messages for us today. We might learn how to make new choices with sagacity by pondering anew her story of triumph and tragedy.

"Defining personality is as frustrating a task as is trying to untie the Gordian knot," psychiatrist Patrick Smallwood once felicitously remarked.[3] As we continue our study of Bible personalities, Elijah is particularly interesting and pertinent. We have often wondered how many of the dear Christians we either see in treatment or minister to are tormented by the imperfections in their personalities. They are committed but not perfect. Venial faults and offenses often cause hours of anguish. Thus, the chapter on Elijah is not to point to the man's perfectionism but rather to show us that God used a wonderful and godly individual in spite of his imperfection. Our clients are not alone in their faults. Elijah was one of only two men in the Bible who never experienced death; he was committed but not perfect. What precepts can we gather from his life? How did God help our imperfect mentor, and what are the take-away messages for us?

And then what shall we do with life's giants—rejection, depression, guilt, opposition, and failure? Will we sink into despair as David did in the early verses of Psalm 32? When faced with life's giants, over 350,000 will attempt suicide this year. The widowed, the divorced, those living alone, the unemployed, and those with severely failing health are all at great risk. Could they discover take-away messages from David and then make fresh choices? David of old offers adages for us today.

David faced many giants, but it seems Job faced even more. No one wants to live Job's story, and yet many of the people we treat or minister to often come close. What are they to do? Some have had suicidal ideations; some have made detailed plans for suicide; some have suffered catastrophes and lost their support systems, leaving them at even greater risk for suicide. And if not suicide, many will become clinically, hopelessly depressed, as Job seemed to do. Can Job help us? Indeed, the book of Job offers valuable maxims for us today—messages that we can apply to our own difficult circumstances.

These paragraphs offer just a few brief vignettes into the first half of *Just Like Us*. In the second half, you will learn take-away messages from the wisest man who ever lived, a peerless king, a prophet of many contrasts, and a mentally healthy man. Then you can discover the challenge of priorities from Martha, learn about the hazards and benefits of risk taking from Peter, and peek into a mental exam of the Apostle Paul.

Why did we choose the Bible characters we did? Were our choices fortuitous, or do they illustrate a panorama of problems people face today? You may wish to ponder the following in considering those questions. Probably 100 percent of people feel ordinary or even inferior in some manner at some time. Thus, studying Gideon is prudent. As many as one in every five people will suffer from a major depressive disorder or other mood disorder during their lives. Studying the nuances of the lives of Moses, Elijah, David, Job, and Jeremiah will assist us in dealing with these issues. Of course, we all want to be successful. Why not learn pearls from Caleb and Hezekiah? Furthermore, since emotional and psychiatric issues such as anxiety disorder or substance abuse may affect almost half of us at some point in our lives, "48 percent of people will experience symptoms of a psychiatric disorder, and during a 12-month period, 29.5 percent of people will exhibit symptoms. Anxiety disorder (24.9 percent over a lifetime and 17.2 percent during a 12-month period) and substance use disorders (26.6 percent over a lifetime and 11.3 percent during a 12-month period) are especially common."[4] Consequently, wouldn't it help us to catch a glimpse into the mental health of David and Paul?

Most Christians have felt a little out of step with society at times, a little idiosyncratic. Can we not be encouraged as we learn from John the Baptist? On the other hand, some believers have struggled with addictions, "besetting sins," or some other kind of

Achilles' heel. Can't we learn from Martha? Certainly we can learn about these struggles from Solomon.

What are the most prominent issues for people today? Among them are feelings of inferiority, discouragement, and depression, as well as conflicts with peers because we are too obsessive or too audacious. We all want mental health and success. Biblical stories encompassing trials and victories speak to every issue we face today. *Just Like Us* elucidates the specifics of those victories.

Finally, why did we choose to order the Bible characters as we did? With the exception of Gideon, the characters are explored according to their order of appearance in the books of the Bible. We wanted to start with an ordinary man, proceed to explore common human frailties and seemingly insurmountable adversities, and then move to remarkable victories. Ordinary people for extraordinary purposes—that was our ultimate guide.

It was around the second millennium B.C., as best we can discern, that the dreaded news of calamity came to Job and he learned the sovereignty of God. You have no doubt identified with the poignant feelings Job must have felt when that series of messages arrived, bringing word of multiple tragedies (Job 1:14, 17, 18). Job's story is still relevant in the twenty-first century.

Moses wrestled with impetuous times and low times circa 1200 B.C. When was the last time you wrestled with the consequences of being impulsive or felt the pain of rebuke? Moses speaks eloquently to help us in 2004.

It was circa 550 B.C. when the following was recorded of Hezekiah: "And the LORD was with him; he was successful in whatever he undertook" (2 Kings 18:7 NIV). He was imperfect but successful. What were his hidden secrets? He offers invaluable adages for today. And Daniel, a gadfly prophet of around 537 B.C., can teach us a lot about obtaining mental health in our modern era.

The lessons from these and the other biblical women and men we've considered are as applicable for us today as when they were written years ago. All the lessons of these biblical stories live today, offering us fresh choices in the pursuit of a life of authentic spirituality—one committed by faith to Jesus Christ, who loved each of us and whose death and resurrection made it possible to experience a life of faith, hope, and love.

Take-away messages from the past and new choices for today are all here for the taking. Our prayer is that you will find them useful and even life-changing.

February 2004   Frank Minirth, M.D.
                                   Don Hawkins, D.Min.
                                   Roy Vogel, Ph.D.

🌿 Just Like Us 🌿

Take-Away Messages from the Past

1. The people of the Bible were just like us, with similar strengths, frailties, and struggles.
2. By studying the lives of biblical characters, we can learn valuable take-away messages from the past that apply today.

Choices for Today

1. Name the one Bible character (other than Christ) you most want to emulate.
2. Name one lesson you want to learn from the Bible character you choose. What choice would you make today to begin to emulate your chosen Bible character?

Acknowledgments

We would like to thank Mary Alice Minirth and Kathy Hawkins for encouragement and patience during the process; Terri Vogel Lavoue for her beauty, character, intellect, and friendship—she is dearly missed by so many; Vickie Gage, Anita Scroggins, and Pam Smith for manuscript typing and administrative assistance; Rebecca Knight and Deanne Easterwood at the Southeastern Bible College Library for research assistance; Allen Bean, Bruce Pickell, Mary Ann Pickell, and Janis Whipple for editing assistance; Bruce Barbour for all his efforts on our behalf; Mark Kerr for believing so strongly in this book; Catherine Craddock and Joanne Clapp Fullagar for shepherding the manuscript through the process at Jossey-Bass; and Sachie Jones and Sandy Siegle for all their marketing help and expertise.

Chapter One

Gideon

An Ordinary Man
with an Extraordinary Purpose

In 1924, English artist William Wolcott came to New York City to record his impressions of that great metropolis. One morning he was visiting in the office of a former colleague when the urge to sketch came over him. Seeing some paper on his friend's desk, he asked if he could use it.

His friend pointed out that the paper he wanted to use wasn't sketching paper. It was just ordinary wrapping paper.

Not wanting to lose that spark of inspiration, Wolcott took the wrapping paper and pointed out to his friend that nothing is ordinary if you know how to use it.

Then on that ordinary wrapping paper Wolcott drew two sketches. Later that year one of them sold for $500, and the other for $1,000—princely sums in 1924. Ordinary wrapping paper in the hands of a great artist became a great masterpiece.

The life of Gideon bears out that truth as well. A friend of Frank Minirth once remarked that Gideon was really just an ordinary person whom God used to do the extraordinary. This remark motivated Frank to study Gideon's life in the biblical record. And the more he studied this man, the more he realized that his friend was right.

When we first meet Gideon in Judges 6, the Midianites were plundering Israel. This had been going on for seven years. Midian was one of the six sons born to Abraham who had been sent east so that only Isaac would inherit the land (approximately seven hundred years earlier). Yet each year about harvest time, Midian's descendants would sweep through Israel, stealing the crops and destroying the people's homes. Conditions had become so bad that the Israelites had taken to living in caves. They were scared to death.

In Judges 6:10 we see the root cause of their predicament. God said through one of his prophets, "Also I said to you, 'I am the LORD your God; do not fear the gods of the Amorites, in whose land you dwell.' But you have not obeyed My voice."

In the book of Judges, we see Israel obeying God for a while and living in happiness and prosperity. Then they would become disobedient, which caused them to end up unhappy and in desperate straits. The Israelites repeated this pattern over and over again: obedience would elevate them; then disobedience would throw them into a tailspin.

Gideon lived during one of these tailspins. The Israelites feared for their lives as well as their livelihoods, and Gideon was right in there with the rest of his people. Judges 6:11–12 says, "Now the Angel of the LORD came and sat under the terebinth tree which was in Ophrah, which belonged to Joash the Abiezrite, while his son Gideon threshed wheat in the winepress, in order to hide it from the Midianites. And the Angel of the LORD appeared to him, and said to him, 'The LORD is with you, you mighty man of valor!'"

Man of valor? Hardly! Here was Gideon, hiding out in a winepress, a depression about three feet deep in a large stone where the grapes were smashed to make wine, hoping to save a little bit of his crops and all of his skin. At this point he could be considered the epitome of human frailty.

But aren't we all? That's the kind of person we can identify with. And that is why God gave us this story of Gideon, an ordinary man, yet one the Lord would make into an extraordinary masterpiece.

Yet the process was not without its challenges. Gideon faced some major roadblocks in becoming the person God intended for him to be, just like many of us do. Let's examine those roadblocks.

Roadblock Number One: Fear

Thirteen-year-old Natalie Gilbert was thrilled to be asked to sing "The Star-Spangled Banner" at a nationally televised NBA Western Conference playoff game. It was a dream come true. On April 25, 2003, Natalie stood alone at center court in Portland's Rose Garden Arena, poised to sing. All around her stood a capacity crowd waiting for her to complete this familiar song so that they could get on with the game. Suddenly, she froze. Her mind blanked. Fear left her wordless. Closing her eyes and shaking her head, she appeared on the verge of tears.

Gideon found himself in the clutches of a similar fear. When we first meet him, Gideon is shaking in his sandals down in a winepress. Paralyzed by the threat of the Midian invaders, the best plan of action Gideon could come up with was to hide and hope his enemies would overlook him.

So why did God choose this ordinary man immobilized by fear? Because that is God's way. We read in 1 Corinthians 1:26–31:

> For you see your calling, brethren, that not many wise according to the flesh, not many mighty, not many noble, are called. But God has chosen the foolish things of the world to put to shame the wise, and God has chosen the weak things of the world to put to shame the things which are mighty; and the base things of the world and the things which are despised God has chosen, and the things which are not, to bring to nothing the things that are, that no flesh should glory in His presence. But of Him you are in Christ Jesus, who became for us wisdom from God—and righteousness and sanctification and redemption—that, as it is written, "He who glories, let him glory in the LORD."

But what about Natalie? The story goes on. As she stood frozen at center court, Maurice Cheeks, the head coach of the Trailblazers, had pity on her. Quickly, he stepped to her side, put his arm around her, and began singing with her. "I didn't even know if I knew all the words, but as many times as I've heard the national anthem, I just went over and continued to sing," Cheeks told *CBS SportsLine*. "The words started coming back to me and I just tried to help her out." And he did. Together they made it all the way through, to "the home of the brave."[1]

That's what God does! When he calls ordinary people to do extraordinary tasks, God does not expect them to do these things on their own. Instead, he comes alongside them in the person of his Spirit and empowers them to do it. It's as the angel reminded Gideon, "The LORD is with you" (Judges 6:12). What God calls us to do, he empowers us through his presence to complete. He breaks through the paralysis of fear and allows us to make it all the way to "the home of the brave." He did that for Gideon; he'll do it for you.

Roadblock Number Two: Doubts

In 1993 FBI agents conducted a raid of the Southwood Psychiatric Hospital in San Diego, which was under investigation for medical insurance fraud. After hours of reviewing medical records, the agents had worked up an appetite. The agent in charge of the in-vestigation called a nearby pizza parlor to order a quick dinner for his colleagues.

According to snopes.com, a Web site dedicated to sleuthing out urban legends, the following telephone conversation actually took place.

Agent: Hello. I would like to order 19 large pizzas and 67 cans of soda.

Pizza man: And where would you like them delivered?

Agent: We're over at the psychiatric hospital.

Pizza man: The psychiatric hospital?

Agent: That's right. I'm an FBI agent.

Pizza man: You're an FBI agent?

Agent: That's correct. Just about everybody here is.

Pizza man: And you're at the psychiatric hospital?

Agent: That's correct. And make sure you don't go through the front doors. We have them locked. You'll have to go around to the back to the service entrance to deliver the pizzas.

Pizza man: And you say you're all FBI agents?

Agent: That's right. How soon can you have them here?

Pizza man: And everyone at the psychiatric hospital is an FBI agent?

Agent: That's right. We've been here all day and we're starving.

Pizza man: How are you going to pay for all of this?

Agent: I have my checkbook right here.

Pizza man: And you're all FBI agents?

Agent: That's right. Everyone here is an FBI agent. Can you remember to bring the pizzas and sodas to the service entrance in the rear? We have the front doors locked.

Pizza man: I don't think so.

[Click.][2]

Circumstances have a way of creating doubts in our minds. They certainly did for Gideon. The angel had just told him, "The LORD is with you" (Judges 6:12). Gideon surely looked down at the paltry sheaf of grain that he held in his hand; he probably looked over at the shallow hole in the stone where he'd been trying to hide. It's totally understandable that he said: "O my lord, if the LORD is with us, why then has all this happened to us? And where are all His miracles which our fathers told us about, saying, 'Did not the LORD bring us up from Egypt?' But now the LORD has forsaken us and delivered us into the hands of the Midianites" (6:13).

God understands about circumstances. That's why Gideon was not fried to a crisp by a heavenly lightning bolt. The angel didn't even rebuke Gideon for his lack of faith. God is open to our doubts. There is no better place to express our doubts than in his presence.

But notice that God also has a solution for our doubts. The Lord replied to Gideon, "Go in this might of yours, and you shall save Israel from the hand of the Midianites. Have I not sent you?" (6:14). Circumstances are open to interpretation (or misinterpretation, as the case may be), but facts are not. No matter what the situation looked like, God had spoken, and that was a fact. Gideon might appeal to circumstances, but God appealed to the facts: "Have I not sent you?"

When faced with doubts, don't look at your situation, look at what God has said—those are the facts. You might feel unloved, but look at the facts in Romans 5:8 ("But God demonstrates His own love toward us, in that while we were still sinners Christ died for us"). You might worry about the future, but look at Jeremiah 29:11, where a promise to Israel of old applies to you today: "For I know the thoughts [plans] that I think toward you, says the LORD, thoughts of peace and not of evil, to give you a future and a hope." You might be wondering if your needs are going to be met, but consider the facts in Philippians 4:19: "And my God shall supply all your need according to his riches in glory by Christ Jesus." Doubts are built on circumstances; faith is based on facts. Look to God's Word for the facts.

Roadblock Number Three: An Inferiority Complex

You may have heard the story of the man who paid a visit to his local psychologist. When the doctor asked him what had prompted the appointment, the man said, "I'm suffering from an inferiority complex." In the ensuing weeks, the psychologist put his new patient through an intensive battery of tests. Next came the long wait while the test results were tabulated and appropriate correlations were made. Finally, the doctor called the man and asked him to return to the clinic. "I have some interesting news for you," the doctor began.

"What's that?" asked the man.

"It's no complex," the psychologist retorted. "You are inferior."

Feelings of inferiority cause a person to focus upon himself or herself. As a psychiatrist, Frank Minirth has seen this with many clients over the years. This is exactly what we see with Gideon. In Judges 6:15 he says: "O my LORD, how can I save Israel? Indeed my clan is the weakest in Manasseh, and I am the least in my father's house." Gideon felt inferior, and he was right. He had all the facts down pat. Indeed, he *was* the least member of his family; his clan *was* the least clan in their tribe; and their tribe *was* the least tribe of Israel. Gideon wasn't suffering from the wrong perception; he was suffering from the wrong perspective. He saw things as they were, but he failed to see them as they could be with God.

It's good to face the facts, but we always need to keep God in the perspective. None of us by nature has what it takes to do the extraordinary tasks God calls us to achieve. But rather than allowing that to give us a woe-is-me attitude, we should allow it to create a wow-is-God attitude.

Being inferior is nothing to get a complex over; we are inferior when it comes to the supernatural resources needed to accomplish God's purposes. But rather than focus on what we can't do in ourselves, we need to focus on what God can do through us. The Apostle Paul says, "I can do all things through Christ who strengthens me" (Philippians 4:13). We can say the same.

Roadblock Number Four: Testing God

In an interview with *Spin*, a music magazine, Scott Stapp, the lead singer of the musical group Creed, discussed the impact his strict religious upbringing had on his life: "I constantly found myself asking God to prove himself. . . . I'd lie in bed and say, 'God, if you're real, just make my light go off so I won't doubt it. I promise I'll be the best Christian in the world.'"[3]

Perhaps the origin of such an idea can be traced all the way back to Gideon. Gideon asked something similar of God as well. Of all the stories in the book of Judges, the story about the fleece is one of the most familiar. In fact, the expression *putting out a fleece* has crept into English to imply setting up a test.

In Judges 6:25–27 God appeared to Gideon a second time, this time in a vision at night. God instructed Gideon to tear down his father's altar to Baal and cut down the wooden image associated with it. In its place he was to build an altar to God and sacrifice a bull from his father's herd, using the wood from the idol as fuel. Gideon did as told, although his fears caused him to do it at night rather than during the day.

Understandably, the townspeople were upset. To make matters worse, all the Midianites and the Amalekites gathered in the Valley of Jezreel to wage war against Israel (vv. 33–34).

Gideon rallied troops from the tribes of Manasseh, Asher, Zebulun, and Naphtali; and God promised to give him victory over his enemies. But he still wasn't sure. Instead, he tested God, asking God to prove whether he was really with Gideon by leaving a wet fleece on dry ground. God knew how weak Gideon's faith was, so God did as Gideon asked. But that one test was not enough for the fragile Gideon. He then asked for another test in which the fleece would be dry and the ground wet! God, ever patient, answered again (vv. 35–40).

Today we often follow the same path Gideon did. We throw out some kind of fleece. We do so by saying, in effect, "God, if this is your will, prove it to me by such and such." In times of weak faith, this may be the best we can do. But a much better way is to find out what God's Word says and place our faith in it. The Bible is far more dependable than some self-designated fleece.

Roadblock Number Five: Tested by God

Some years ago at Ohio State University in a huge lecture hall, approximately one thousand students were completing a calculus final. The calculus teacher was not well liked. He was one of those people who would stand at the front of the class and yell out how much time was remaining before the students' doom was sealed. At the end he would have the students stack the incomplete tests on a huge podium at the front of the room. With a thousand students in the class, this made for quite a mess.

During this particular final, one student who took the test needed a decent grade to pass the class. His only problem with calculus was that he did poorly when rushed, and this instructor standing in the front of the room barking out how much time was left before the tests had to be handed in didn't help him at all. Wanting to assure himself of a good grade, he hardly flinched when the professor said, "Pencils down and submit your Scantron sheets and work to piles at the front of the room." Long after the test was officially over, as the professor prepared to pick up the test papers and leave, the student finally put down his pencil, gathered up his work, and headed to the front of the hall to submit his final.

"What do you think you're doing?" the professor asked as the student stood in front of him about to put down his exam on one of the neatly stacked piles of exams.

"Turning in my exam," retorted the student confidently.

"I'm afraid I have some bad news for you," the professor gloated, "your exam is late. You've failed it; and consequently, I'll see you next term when you repeat my course."

The student smiled slyly and asked the professor, "Do you know who I am?"

"No," snarled the professor.

The student looked the professor dead in the eyes and said slowly, "I didn't think so," as he lifted up one of the stacks halfway and shoved his test neatly into the center of the stack. Then he turned around and walked casually out of the huge lecture hall.[4]

Neither Gideon nor we have any such hope of anonymity. The Lord knows each one of us, and just as surely as God builds our faith through answered prayer, he will also test our faith. We see that with Gideon.

After all, Gideon was already outnumbered. The Midianites had perhaps 135,000 men in their army (Judges 8:10), whereas

Gideon's army numbered about thirty-two thousand. The odds were four to one! However, it was possible even with those odds that people might say Gideon had achieved victory in his own strength. So God told Gideon to let everyone in his army who was afraid go home. Only twenty-two thousand men were left. That made the odds six to one. Most of us would have thought of leaving with that first group of ten thousand. The odds, however, still allowed for Gideon's soldiers to get the glory. So God told Gideon to test his men to see who would remain. Gideon led the men to a stream to get a drink of water. Those who lapped the water like dogs were told to remain; the rest were sent home (7:5–7). That left Gideon with an army of only three hundred. The odds were now more than four hundred to one—just God's kind of battle!

Don't be surprised if God tests you. We've seen that God comforts us when we are weak, yet he will also put us in circumstances that will test us and thus build us up. If you have a weak area in your life, be assured God loves you and will comfort you. But be prepared for him to test you as he takes you from being an ordinary person to one who can accomplish extraordinary tasks for him.

What Lies Ahead?

We have seen where Gideon came from. We've examined his roadblocks. Let's now consider his destination.

On a night in about 1400 B.C. we find Gideon's small band of soldiers on a hilltop surveying the Midianites' vast army. You would think that by now Gideon would have confidence in God. But this was not the case; he was still scared to death. God again showed tremendous love, patience, and understanding. He permitted Gideon to slip down into the Midianites' camp and hear a man relaying a dream to a comrade, one that assured Gideon of victory (see Judges 7:9–14 for details).

Bolstered by this assurance, Gideon gathered his men. He gave each a trumpet, a torch, and a pitcher in which to hide the torch. They surrounded the Midianites. Then under Gideon's direction, they blew their trumpets in unison, broke the pitchers, held up their torches and shouted, "The sword of the LORD and of Gideon" (7:20). They must have appeared to number in the thousands. The Midianites were startled, and a mass suicidal and even homicidal panic ensued. Quickly, it was over. God had used the likes of Gideon—an ordinary man just like you and me—to accomplish an extraordinary purpose: the liberating of the people of Israel from Midianite oppression.

God desires to do the same for us today. He wants to put you and me on the hill, surrounding the Midianites, facing odds of four hundred to one.

How does God take ordinary people and have them accomplish extraordinary purposes for him? One of the keys can be found in Judges 6:34: "the Spirit of the LORD came upon Gideon." Zechariah 4:6 states, " 'Not by might, nor by power, but by my Spirit,' says the LORD of hosts." This should cause us to take heart because God still does the same for us today. You see, it is not what we can accomplish for God; rather, it is what God can do through us. The same Spirit is as available to work through us today as he was in the day of Gideon.

The late Bill Bright, founder of Campus Crusade for Christ, often told how he began his career as a "happy pagan, working to promote a food business that he had initiated." But then God got hold of his life. In 1945 Dr. Bright gave his heart to Christ. By 1951 he and his wife, Vonette, knew God wanted to do something extraordinary in their lives. They drew up a contract joyfully renouncing their earthly interests in order to give themselves to advancing the "Great Commission" (God's mandate to spread the message of Christ throughout the world). That was the beginning of what was to become the world's largest Christian ministry, Campus Crusade for Christ, which now serves people in 191 countries with a staff of twenty-six thousand full-time employees. In 1956 Dr. Bright wrote a booklet entitled "The Four Spiritual Laws," whose more than 2.5 billion copies have been printed in two hundred languages.[5] In 1979 he commissioned the film *Jesus*, now the most widely viewed film in history, with more than 5.1 billion viewers in 234 countries.[6] All this from an ordinary business man who became an extraordinary tool in God's hands.

Don't let the roadblocks become stumbling blocks. God can make something extraordinary out of you.

🌿 Gideon 🌿

Take-Away Messages from the Past

1. We all feel ordinary.
2. We are all afraid at times.
3. We all have doubts and questions.
4. We all test God at times. God also may test us periodically.
5. God can permit circumstances today in which the odds against you are four hundred to one.

Choices for Today

1. Even though you may be ordinary, how has God chosen you for an extraordinary purpose? What choices can you make today to further the fulfillment of this purpose?
2. Name one circumstance you faced recently when you experienced fear. What choice can you make today to decrease your fear?
3. What one choice could you make today to help you with your doubts and questions?
4. Do you feel like God may be testing you? How could you choose to cooperate with him and succeed in turning the test into a victory?
5. Can you name a specific circumstance today in which you took a stand for God and faced tremendous odds? Have you chosen, by his grace and in his way, to win?

Chapter Two

Job

Reacting to Multiple Trials

Life has a way of dealing people some very difficult blows. The obituary of Colonel Floyd J. Thompson documents one example. According to this brief summary, Colonel Thompson endured for nine years "cold cells, jungle cages, and torture in Vietnam, becoming the longest-serving American prisoner of war in any conflict." He died July 16, 2002, at age sixty-nine.

The citation that accompanied his Distinguished Service Medal said "Jimmy" Thompson had endured "unfathomable deprivation and hardship" in the service of his country.

Perhaps the most arresting paragraph in his obituary was this: "'Dying is easy,' an enemy camp commander told him. 'Living is the difficult thing.'"

The obituary revealed how true that was in Colonel Thompson's case. He was released from his nine-year captivity on March 16, 1973. After he returned home, he was divorced twice, battled alcoholism and depression, and suffered a stroke in 1981 that put him in a coma for six months and left him partly paralyzed.[1]

When we look at a person like Colonel Thompson, we have to wonder how well we would have handled similar trials. And that's when it helps us to focus our attention on a man named Job. Down through the ages, this patriarch has been associated with trials and suffering. People have turned to the book of Job more than to any other for answers in responding to times of difficulty.

Ezekiel 14:14, 20 and James 5:11 (KJV, where we find the famous "patience of Job") make passing references to Job. But most of
what we know about Job comes from the book of Job itself. He was
from the land of Uz, which is the same territory as Edom (Lamentations 4:21) located southeast of the Dead Sea. The biblical evidence
also seems to indicate that he lived around 2000 B.C. Several facts
support this: (1) he lived more than 140 years (Job 42:16), a life
span consistent with the patriarchal period; (2) there is no reference
to the nation of Israel or the Mosaic Law (both of which came into
existence about 1500 B.C.).

The book of Job (1:3 KJV) also reveals that he was "the greatest of all the men of the east." This may be a reference to his vast
wealth. Here was a man who started out with great wealth (Job 1)
and ended up with even greater wealth (Job 42). But we can't dis-
count the fact that Job was great in the sense of being not only very
moral but godly (1:1, 5). In fact, his godliness became the cause of
Satan's challenge before God.

But before we consider this challenge, we should point out that
the book of Job does not revolve around the question of why the
godly suffer. Other scriptural passages answer this question: to discipline God's children (Hebrews 12), to demonstrate the power of
Christ (2 Corinthians 12), to keep down pride (2 Corinthians 12),
to manifest the works of God (John 9), due to the sins of others
(Hosea 1), because of the fall of man (Genesis 3), to develop patience (Romans 5), and to demonstrate the glory of Christ (1 Peter 1).
But the cause of suffering isn't the focal point of Job's story. Rather
than giving the cause (in fact, God never tells Job why he had to
suffer as he did), the emphasis of the book of Job is on how a godly
person should respond to those trials.

What makes this biblical book so valuable is that it records the
profound lessons Job learned as a result of the many trials he experienced. Through all his tribulations, he learned to react appropriately to adversity. These lessons are as valid today as when they
were given millennia ago, because these same trials are still with us
and God is still the same.

Satan's Challenge

As we delve into the book of Job, we discover Satan standing before God to accuse the patriarch of serving the Lord for wealth, to obtain the material blessings he received (1:9–10). Consequently, God gives Satan permission to rob Job of his ten children and his wealth. Yet Job shows great spiritual strength at this point: "Then Job arose, tore his robe, and shaved his head; and he fell to the ground and worshiped. And he said: 'Naked I came from my mother's womb, and naked shall I return there. The LORD gave, and the LORD has taken away; blessed be the name of the LORD.' In all this Job did not sin nor charge God with wrong" (1:20–22).

Next, Satan accuses Job of serving God for his own welfare. Consequently, God permits Satan to take away even Job's health. Job 2:7 reveals, "So Satan went out from the presence of the LORD, and struck Job with painful boils from the sole of his foot to the crown of his head."

Finally, this servant of the Lord began to break: "After this Job opened his mouth and cursed the day of his birth" (Job 3:1).

What would possess a man to do that, especially a man whom God described as "blameless and upright; who feared God and shunned evil" (1:1)? A person who has just lost all his possessions, his children, his servants, his support system (everyone abandoned him in his hour of need), and finally his health (covered from head to toe with boils, he sat on an ash heap scraping himself with a broken piece of pottery) could surely say worse things.

A careful reading of the book of Job, however, also shows us that this godly man was suffering from severe depression. In today's clinical terminology, we might say he was suffering from a major depressive disorder. It could also be noted that the depression was reactive in nature, meaning that it was clearly triggered by external circumstances—in this case involving multiple losses of catastrophic proportions. Given a depression of this magnitude, most mental health professionals today would pursue hospital admission and treatment as the most appropriate level of care.

Symptoms of Depression

Job demonstrated virtually every major symptom of depression. His mood was intensely depressed nearly every minute of the day over a period of months. The normal activities of daily living did not interest him at all; nothing in life was pleasurable for him anymore. His appetite was virtually nonexistent, and he had become emaciated. He suffered from severe insomnia. Agitation was a constant companion. Far beyond common levels of fatigue, he experienced a profound loss of energy; he couldn't even raise himself up off the ash heap.

Although in some ways his mind was still functioning at a high level, Job's ability to think in a normal manner had become severely impaired, to the point where all he could think of was his anguish. Job considered his entire life to have been worthless. Who could blame him? As it turned out, his best friends and everyone else who knew him blamed him, and some even shunned him. Job did not fear death; he yearned for it. He repeatedly expressed strong feelings of hopelessness and an intense desire to die.

Clearly, Job proves that a man could be "blameless and upright, a man who fears God and shuns evil" (1:1) and suffer from a severe clinical depression at the same time. A myth common in Christian circles says this is not possible. This myth has done a great deal of damage to many people. Consequently, we need to remember that if a severe depression could happen to a godly man like Job, it or any other emotional ailment could happen to anyone. Let's take a closer look at Job's depression.

Job's Level of Depression

How depressed was Job? He had many of the symptoms of clinical depression seen in depressed individuals today. Consider the following:

- Job said his anguish, if it could be weighed, "would surely outweigh the sand of the seas" (6:3 NIV).

- "My eyes will never see happiness again" (7:7 NIV).
- "I despise my life; I would not live forever" (7:16 NIV).
- "Why have you made me your target?" (7:20b NIV).
- "I do not believe he would give me a hearing" (9:16b NIV).
- "Why should I struggle in vain?" (9:29b NIV).
- "I loathe my very life" (10:1a NIV).
- "Why then did you bring me out of the womb?" (10:18 NIV).

Clearly, Job was severely depressed. Yet the plot thickened even more as Job's wife and four friends offered their answers as to why people suffer. First, Job's wife expressed what might seem to be a logical explanation: God is just unfair. Job dealt with her well, pointing out that it is unreasonable to expect God to allow only good things and no calamities for those who live in a fallen world (2:10).

Later his friends arrived and sat silently for seven days, listening to Job's lamentations. Job spoke out of physical and mental anguish, and it showed. Then his friends responded. Three of the four friends offered another popular view of suffering: all suffering is due to sin.[2] They felt Job was a hypocrite. They also saw God as petty and exacting in his relations with humankind. In addition, they were dogmatic in proclaiming their position. They would have fared much better if they had continued their initial course of being present but remaining silent (2:13).

The fourth friend, Elihu, seemed to possess the most wisdom: "I said, 'Age should speak, and multitude of years should teach wisdom.' But there is a spirit in man, and the breath of the Almighty gives him understanding. Great men are not always wise, nor do the aged always understand justice" (Job 32:7–9). "Behold, God is exalted by His power, who teaches like Him? Who has assigned Him His way, or who has said, 'You have done wrong'?" (Job 36:22–23).

Elihu felt that suffering was a means of purifying the righteous and bringing that person to a place of complete trust in God (33:29–30). Although Elihu showed more wisdom than Job's three other friends, his wisdom was far from complete. (Examples of this can be seen in 35:9–16, where he too provides a simplistic answer to Job's dilemma—the patriarch, he charges, has "multiplied words without knowledge" in response to his adversity, without properly acknowledging his creator.)

In summary, the disasters Job experienced are found in the first two chapters; the rest of the book records the dialogues between Job and his friends.

Let's focus on Job 42, where we find the heart of the lesson of this man and the book that bears his name. Here we discover the principles that God wants to teach us concerning how to react to trials.

Your Reactions Are Showing

First, we discover that God wants us to respond in confidence because he is in control. Job declares, "I know that You can do everything, and that no purpose of Yours can be withheld from You" (42:2). After God took Job on a mental tour of the universe and the animal kingdom, the patriarch began to appreciate God's power. If God was able to control a universe containing millions of galaxies with at least one of those galaxies so large that crossing it while traveling at the speed of light would take one hundred thousand years, then he should be able to control the trials in our lives. If God has power over the animal kingdom, then he certainly has power over the tribulations that come into our lives as well. God is always in control of everything, so we can trust him even when we do not understand all of life.

Second, we learn that God's intelligence is far above our intelligence. Job admits, "'Who is this who hides counsel without knowledge?' Therefore I have uttered what I did not understand, things too wonderful for me, which I did not know" (42:3). God's ways are far beyond our comprehension. Our IQ is finite; his IQ is infinite. Compare an ant's intelligence to our intelligence, and you have somewhat of an analogy of our intelligence compared to God's. However, even this analogy falls short, because the ant would be so much smarter in comparison to us than we are in comparison to God. But our confidence is that if God is so vastly more intelligent, we certainly can trust that God is too intelligent to make a mistake.

Third, we learn the importance of moving from head knowledge to personal experience. Job confessed: "I have heard of You by the hearing of the ear, but now my eye sees You" (42:5). Our knowledge of God may be merely hearsay. Perhaps we were raised in a Christian home, in which we constantly heard about God. This isn't bad, but we need the experimental teaching and revelation of God himself so that we can see with an inward eye and really know him. The Scriptures imply that Job certainly knew God (1:1) but not to the depth he later came to know God (42:5).

Finally, we learn that we need a change of mind. In humility Job declares, "Therefore I abhor myself, and repent in dust and ashes" (42:6). Repentance means a change of mind. When Job reached the depth of knowledge of God, he no longer had to know why God had allowed the trials. His thinking about God, and about himself and his circumstances, had truly been changed. Often we accuse God falsely when he allows trials to come into our lives. We call into question God's love for us, his wisdom, and even his power. We need to repent, as did Job, of such foolishness.

Not Why but What

In his book, *In the Eye of the Storm*, Max Lucado tells the true story of Chippie the parakeet. It seems that Chippie's owner decided to clean the birdcage with a vacuum cleaner. Taking off the attachment, she stuck it in the cage. Then the phone rang.

As she bent down to answer the phone, she heard a "sssopp" noise and realized she had accidentally sucked Chippie into the vacuum cleaner. She quickly opened the bag and, amazingly enough, the bird was stunned but still alive.

Noticing that he was covered with dust and dirt, she grabbed him and raced to the bathroom, turned on the faucet and held Chippie under the running water.

Realizing that Chippie was soaked and shivering, she did what any compassionate bird owner would do: she reached for the hair dryer and blasted her pet with hot air until he was dry.

A few days after all this, a friend called to see how Chippie was getting along. "Well," the bird owner replied, "Chippie is still alive—but he doesn't sing much anymore. He just sits and stares."[3]

There are days when we may feel like Chippie: sucked in, washed up, blown over, and unable to sing. And the temptation is to ask, "Why, God?"

But God is more concerned that we ask "What, God? What do you want me to learn about reacting to these trials?" We can find the answers in Job. Job was the greatest man of his time but not because he was rich or even because he was moral and godly. Though he was all those things, his real greatness was in his ability to get out of his trials what God intended that he learn—particularly the truths of God's sovereign care and personal compassion.

🍃 Job 🍃

Take-Away Messages from the Past

Job learned how to react to trials:

1. Realize God is still in control.
2. Realize God's intelligence is far greater than our intelligence.
3. Realize we need to move from just head knowledge to a personal experience of God.
4. Realize we need to repent of foolish responses to our trials.

Choices for Today

1. Of these four lessons on reacting to trials, which one do you relate to the most? Would you be willing to memorize Job 42:5: "I have heard of You by the hearing of the ear, but now my eye sees You"?

2. Choose to respond to the suffering of others as Job's friends did initially: be present and supportive, but don't sermonize.

3. When you are seeking to support someone who feels depressed due to adversity, avoid the kind of discouraging comments Job's wife offered, or the simplistic platitudes of his friends.

Chapter Three

Moses

A Man of Ups and Downs

Is your life characterized by ups and downs? Perhaps you do well at times, even very well, but then at other times you find yourself really down. You can learn valuable insights and new choices from Moses.

Of all the biblical characters we tend to elevate to superhuman level, perhaps Moses is the one we are inclined to lift the highest. Hollywood productions such as *The Ten Commandments* are partly responsible. Mention the name *Moses* and many people think of Charlton Heston, ten feet tall on the silver screen, spreading his arms over the Red Sea while horses and chariots are swept away.

Yet Moses was not a character created by Cecil B. DeMille. He was a person, a real-life individual just like us, a man whose human struggles were tempered by the fact that God used him wonderfully. His was a life of peaks and valleys, just like ours. As we examine some facets of Moses' life and personality, we can learn take-away messages that will enable us to cope with some of the struggles we face today.

As we examine the biblical record of Moses' life, we can't help noticing how his life was marked by cycles. He certainly experienced times of greatness, exuberance, leadership, courage, and decisiveness. Just think of the burning bush, his series of confrontations with Pharaoh, the strategic victory over the Egyptians at the Red Sea, the decisive conquest over the Amalekites, and the giving of the Law at Sinai. Yet he also experienced valleys: his murder of the Egyptian, his attempted refusal to become God's spokesman at age eighty, his frequent bouts with depression, and the anger he expressed in disobeying

God by striking the rock to produce water (Numbers 20:11, 12). Perhaps your life, like Moses' own, has been marked by both.

Many people today find their lives marked by significant ups and downs. For example, it has been estimated that as much as 1 percent of the population in North America is affected by a major affective (mood) disorder called bipolar disorder.[1] Bipolar individuals experience periods of euphoria similar to those of amphetamine users. They feel intensely cheerful and self-confident even to the point of judgment impairment; they often demonstrate intense energy and rapid speech. The depressive side of bipolar disorder is marked by moods that drop to intense sadness, an appearance of depression, painful thinking, and even suicidal thoughts.

A less intense form of ups and downs, perhaps one similar to what Moses experienced, is what modern psychology refers to as cyclothymic personality disorder, a "pervasive pattern of pronounced periodic changes in mood, behavior, thinking, sleep and energy levels . . . [alternating] between over-optimism or exaggeration of past achievement and a pessimistic attitude toward the future."[2] Individuals with this disorder experience periods of low self-esteem alternating with periods of inflated self-esteem, a pessimistic attitude alternating with overoptimism, periods of inability to concentrate or think clearly alternating with periods of sharpened and unusually creative thinking. At times persons with cyclothymic disorder exhibit high-spirited brilliance, energy, and creativity alternating with gloom and pessimism.

In examining the life of Moses, we see that, to some degree, he experienced such alternating swings of mood, energy, and ability. In other words, like the cyclothymic individual today, Moses lived a life of peaks and valleys.

Rescued from the Nile

Anyone who has spent any extended time in Sunday school has heard about Moses' fascinating early life. In fact, his birth and early life actually could be considered his first peak! Born in the darkest point of the history of the Israelites, his very name vividly describes God's sovereign care during the early events of his life. The name *Moses* means "drawn out," and that's exactly what happened to him shortly after his birth.

For approximately four hundred years, the Israelites had experienced great blessings in Egypt. Their population had grown to perhaps two million or more. The Egyptian pharaoh implemented a strategy to limit the Israelite birthrate by putting male children to death. Foiled by loyal Jewish midwives who chose to obey God rather than the king, Pharaoh ordered that every newborn male Israelite be "cast into the river" (Exodus 1:22). Against the backdrop of this cruel edict, the faith of Moses' natural parents is highlighted by Hebrews 11:23. His father, Amram, and his mother, Jochebed (Exodus 6:20), were both Levites, members of the tribe that would ultimately lead in the worship of the true God. Though living in a pagan, idolatrous atmosphere that ran counter to their faith, Moses' parents somehow maintained their commitment to the God of Israel. Their faith produced a confidence in God's hand of protection that enabled them not to fear the king (Hebrews 11:23). For over ninety days after Moses' birth, his parents were preoccupied with protecting their beautiful son's life.

Yet the day came when they could no longer hide Moses. The strategy that Jochebed devised was divinely ironic, and Moses was placed in an ark near the river bank. Ultimately, the Nile River, which had been the place of death for so many Israelite babies, became the key to preserving Moses' life. Discovered and claimed by Pharaoh's daughter at the river bank, Moses was adopted into the royal family; and God's hand of protection was evident when Pharaoh's daughter appointed his birth mother, Jochebed, as his nurse!

Thus, Moses' early years—those years that shape so many of our attitudes and values—were years dramatically crafted by God and spent under the influence of godly Jewish parents. This helped to prepare Moses for the pagan environment in which he would find himself. Perhaps, like Moses, you were blessed to have been born to godly parents, raised in a church that taught the Bible, or attended a Christian camp where you were challenged to give your life to the Lord. If so, don't forget to thank him.

Like many individuals who wind up in significant positions of leadership—such as presidents John F. Kennedy and the two George Bushes—Moses experienced significant advantages in his early life. God allowed him to be born a physically handsome or beautiful individual (Exodus 2:2; Hebrews 11:23). According to the Jewish historian Josephus, Moses was a young man of such outstanding appearance that "his charm captivated passersby," and the Egyptians would often run after him just to try to catch a glimpse of him, in much the same way people respond to popular movie stars or athletes today.[3] In addition to his physical abilities, Moses undoubtedly possessed a genius-level mind. He absorbed all the education Egypt had to offer. Furthermore, he was a gifted communicator. Stephen referred to him as "powerful in speech and action" (Acts 7:22 NIV). The Jewish historian Josephus further documented his leadership ability, telling how, after Moses had been appointed general over the Egyptian army, he turned impending defeat at the hands of Ethiopia into a great Egyptian victory.[4] Perhaps you don't have the genius-level intelligence or dramatic leadership skills of Moses or even his outstanding good looks; yet God has gifted each of us in some way, and we all need to pause to recognize that giftedness and thank God for it.

Two Strategic Decisions

Near the fortieth year of his life, Moses made two strategic choices that set the stage for the rest of his life. One of those choices is recorded in Hebrews 11:25: Moses chose to endure ill treatment with the people of God rather than enjoy the passing pleasures of sin. With all the prerogatives of a pagan prince at his disposal, with the opportunity to sample every sensual pleasure imaginable, at the height of his career, Moses reflected on his Hebrew heritage and how the faith of his godly parents could and should make the difference in his life. Then he determined to identify with his own people, even at the risk of experiencing suffering, rather than maintain his royal position as the son of Pharaoh's daughter. So even though he could have very well become the pharaoh of Egypt, Moses set his course decisively toward his parents' people and their God.

Life confronts many of us with just such a decision, and our lives can take a turn toward God and his purposes or away from him, depending on the choice we make. For a young man we know named Wayne, that decisive moment came during his junior year in high school. His guidance counselor had called Wayne in to tell him about a new program through which gifted high school students could bypass their senior year and go straight to college. Wayne had several offers to consider, opportunities for scholarships to several prestigious schools, including a couple from Ivy League universities.

Over the weekend Wayne and his godly parents prayed about the decision. On Monday he announced his choice, to the shock and chagrin of his guidance counselor and teachers: "I believe God is calling me into ministry. I would like to use this program to attend a Bible college," he explained. Ultimately, Wayne wound up in the pastorate. His high school teachers may have considered his decision a waste, but spiritually, he was right on target.

For Marty, a man whom Don Hawkins met at a business luncheon and later discipled, the choice came well into his career at a successful investment brokerage. Marty had been a Christian since his teenage years, but when he began studying God's Word and growing spiritually, he realized he needed to make major changes to restore integrity to his business practices. Unfortunately, a man at his firm whom Marty had helped to train disagreed with his newly adopted value system and its contrast with the way his associates continued to treat their clients. Ultimately, Marty was fired. He had made a tough choice but one that demonstrated how he had become a man of godly character.

Perhaps you have been confronted by similar choices in your life. On the one hand, you find yourself attracted to the pleasures, prosperity, and enjoyable things life has to offer. On the other hand, you may take a hit financially, lose the esteem of friends and colleagues, even find yourself misunderstood and persecuted. Let us encourage you to weigh the balance sheet as Moses did. According to Hebrews 11:26, he "esteemed the reproach of Christ greater riches than the treasures in Egypt; for he looked to the reward." Perhaps as you read those words you wondered, *What possible reward could he have been considering?* After all, Egypt was the wealthiest nation on earth at that time, and all its treasures were at Moses' disposal.

Frankly, the reward Moses considered went well beyond things material. He was considering what Woodrow Kroll, senior Bible teacher on the *Back to the Bible* radio broadcast, frequently affirms from his own experience and encourages others to follow. According to Dr. Kroll, in numerous radio broadcasts Don Hawkins co-hosted, it's always best to begin every day at the judgment seat of Christ, then work backward toward that specific day and its choices. From what the author of Hebrews said, Moses was able to see beyond the temporal and focus on the eternal. At this critical watershed in his life, he established decisive priorities; and in a vivid illustration of what Paul would later label "reasonable service" for believers (Romans 12:1), Moses committed his life to God.

Whether you're in those formative high school or college years or well into your career, it's never too late to come to that decisive point of turning your life, your goals, and your dreams over to the Savior who loved you and gave himself for you.

A Do-It-Yourself Choice

Shortly after deciding to identify with God's plan and people, Moses made another choice—and the results were tragic. It ultimately produced a great deal of grief and led to his spending forty years tending sheep in the wilderness. Moses had just committed his life to being identified with God's people when he faced one of the thousands of daily injustices the Egyptians brought against the Israelites. Moses almost sacrificed his future on the altar of the present by impulsively killing the Egyptian taskmaster who was persecuting one of his fellow Hebrews (Exodus 2:11, 12). It was as if Moses had plunged off the top of a roller-coaster into a deep valley. In his sermon in Acts 7, Stephen gave a divinely inspired glimpse into Moses' motivation in this hasty act and the one that occurred the following day: "He supposed that his brethren would have understood that God would deliver them by his hand, but they did not understand" (Acts 7:25). About twenty-four hours later, when Moses attempted to mediate between two Israelites who were embroiled in conflict, they both turned on him (7:27)! Perhaps their question—"Who made you a ruler and judge over us?"—set the stage for Moses' serious self-doubts and the questions he would express to God forty years later (Exodus 4). Prompted by fear, Moses again responded impulsively; he fled for his life to Midian (2:15).

Perhaps, like Moses, you have found yourself riding the crest of success, enjoying the aftermath of a successful decision, when suddenly you've been confronted by one of those no-win situations. Like Moses, your heart was in the right place, but your hasty action threw your life into chaos. Perhaps this occurred years ago, and you assumed God had given up on you. He hasn't. God specializes in extending second chances to those who make unwise decisions. He did with Moses, and he will with you. You see, even though Moses found himself tending sheep on the back side of the desert, the God David labeled "my Shepherd" (Psalm 23:1) was still watching over Moses as he tended his flock. God was using those years to sand away some of the rough edges in Moses' personality, just as he uses the daily grind to accomplish his purpose in our lives. So if you think God has given up on you, think again. He delights in taking us back from the valley to another mountain peak.

The Burning Bush

The scene could be something out of a Steven Spielberg movie. Moses, nearing the age of eighty, was tending his sheep in Midian. Forty years had passed, when suddenly one day "an Angel of the Lord appeared to him in a flame of fire in a bush, in the wilderness of Mount Sinai" (Acts 7:30). Those simple facts, recited centuries later by Stephen in a sermon, don't do justice to the awesome impact of that event. When Moses awakened that morning, he wasn't thinking, *Now, this is going to be one of the greatest days of my life!* But sometimes God catches us by surprise. He did with Moses, and he certainly can with us.

In the record Moses himself wrote many years later, he recorded his response: "I will now turn aside and see this great sight, why the bush does not burn" (Exodus 3:3). When he did, God called his name twice—a frequent device in Scripture when the Lord wants to get someone's attention. If you look carefully through Scripture, you will find seven occasions when the Lord repeats someone's name. It happened to Abraham, Moses, and Samuel in the Old Testament; and to the residents of Jerusalem, Martha, Peter, and Saul of Tarsus in the New Testament. If you take the time to examine each incident (a worthwhile pursuit), you'll discover some important facets of God's interest in attracting our attention to him and his purposes in our lives.[5]

That's what God was doing at this point in Moses' life in an incredible demonstration of his power and holiness. After Moses had spent forty years on the end of the bench, the Lord was calling him and sending him into the huddle to call the plays for the Israelites so that they could successfully move from Egypt to their promised land.

Perhaps, like Moses, you are well beyond midlife. You wonder, *Could God be calling me to some kind of specific service?* The answer, quite frankly, could be yes. Don's friends Kelly and Donna invested decades in the secular workplace. They weren't getting rich, but they lived comfortably, and they served faithfully in their local church. Then one day they both sensed God was calling them to a different ministry. They left their jobs and began serving Christian organizations, doing everything from maintenance to heading construction projects. Their story could be told many times over by individuals who have moved from the height of a job or career—or for that matter a layoff prompted by job downsizing—to Bible college or seminary to train for ministry; or to the mission field, the pastorate, or some other area of Christian service. Just because you spent the last forty years working at a factory or tending a flock doesn't mean God doesn't have a big job just ahead for you.

Objection After Objection

Ironically, when God spelled out his plan for Moses and the Israelites—explaining that he had seen the oppression of the Israelites, that he planned to deliver them, and that Moses would be his instrument of choice (Exodus 3:7–10)—Moses' response was shocking, though not totally unexpected. Throughout the third and fourth chapters of Exodus, he raised one objection after another—even though God was speaking to him from a burning bush! One of the difficulties we often face today is that, like Moses, we find it difficult to see things from God's perspective rather than from a human viewpoint. Through the burning bush, the Lord was presenting Moses with an important lesson: he had tried to deliver the Israelites through his own power forty years earlier and failed. For decades he'd had ample time to reflect on his failure. Yet God decisively intervened through the burning bush to point out that Moses had the Lord's inexhaustible resources at his disposal.

In his initial response to God, Moses demonstrated the kind of struggles with self-image with which most of us can identify. He raised the question, "Who am I?" (3:11). God's response was both interesting and significant for us. The Lord didn't tell Moses how good he was or that he just needed to love himself more. Instead, he assured his servant that he'd be right with him, every step of the way. It seemed that Moses missed the point altogether. He seems to have been bent on turning this spiritual peak into a valley. "Who am I?" he began. "I'll be with you," the Lord replied. The issue isn't "Who are you?" It's "Who sent you?"

"What shall I tell them when they ask who you are?" Moses asked next (we're paraphrasing the conversation recorded in Scripture).

"I AM," God replied. "Just tell them, I AM sent you."

"What if they refuse to believe me or listen to me?" Moses countered.

"No problem," God replied. "I'll authenticate your message with three miraculous signs: a rod that turns into a snake, a hand that turns leprous, and water from the Nile that will turn into blood."

"OK, Lord, I'm ready to go," Moses responded. You'd think so, but as a matter of fact, he still wasn't ready to say yes.

"Lord I'm not eloquent," he complained next. Ironically, Stephen later referred to Moses as a man "mighty in words and deeds" (Acts 7:22).

But God didn't condemn Moses or say, "Perhaps you are a bit rusty—after all, you've only been talking to sheep these past forty years." Instead, the Lord raised the real underlying question: "Who has made man's mouth? . . . Have not I, the LORD?" (Exodus 4:11). The lesson for us is clear. The same God who made each of us can gift us and empower us to carry out extraordinary acts of service for him, acts that are well beyond our normal human abilities.

But Moses still wasn't ready to serve—in fact, his final objection prompted an angry response from God. He basically said, "LORD, please send someone else to do it" (4:13 NIV). So God sent Aaron, which proved to be a short-term blessing and a long-term source of frustration, because ultimately Moses was God's choice for the task at hand.

So what was the problem here? Moses desperately needed to learn three lessons. First, as he had affirmed in his decision years before, his life belonged to God. He was, at this point, to be Israel's messiah, the one anointed to lead the Israelites out, and in so doing to foreshadow the ultimate role of Jesus Christ. Second, he needed to learn the lesson Paul affirms for us in Philippians 4:13: "I can do all things through Christ who strengthens me." Third, he needed to learn the lesson of balance. At age forty he had said, "I can handle it, no problem." At age eighty his response to the challenge was "I can't do it at all."

Recently, the three authors of this book have spent a lot of time thinking about the lesson Moses learned, a lesson Paul explains in terms of service to the Lord today. It's a lesson that applies whether you are involved in vocational ministry as a pastor or missionary or serve in a lay capacity. In 2 Corinthians 2:16 the apostle, while discussing the life-and-death ministry of the gospel, asks, "And who is sufficient for these things?" He answers his question a few verses later, noting, "Not that we are sufficient of ourselves to think of anything as being from ourselves, but our sufficiency is from God" (3:5). The point is obvious: there are tasks to be done, ministry to carry out. We can't do them ourselves. When we find our sufficiency in him, we can.

Stability in Peaks and Valleys

Throughout the life of Moses, we see remarkable high points, which demonstrate his stability and steadfastness under pressure. His dramatic confrontation with Pharaoh during the series of plagues, his leadership of the Israelites exhibited at the Passover and the incredible Red Sea crossing, his role as God's instrument when the Lord provided water from the rock and victory over the Amalekites (Exodus 17), and of course his role as the mediator delivering God's detailed revelation to Israel at Mt. Sinai are among the peaks in Moses' ministry performance.

Moses exhibited a great deal of stability under stress and in most of his "valley" experiences. For example, when the Israelites murmured just three days after the successful Red Sea crossing, Moses cried out to God in response to the bitterness of the people (Exodus 15:22–27). Later, facing the pressure of overwork due to the demands of millions of people under his responsibility, Moses listened to his father-in-law's advice and developed a system for delegating all but the most important matters to others (Exodus 18). When the Israelites disobeyed God and made and worshiped a golden calf, Moses' response to God's offer to "consume them" and "make of you a great nation" was to intercede for Israel, to whom he referred as "Your people" (Exodus 32:11). When some of the people expressed jealousy because others besides Moses gave evidence of

God's miraculous work in their lives, the patriarch's response was a gracious and appropriate: "Oh that all the LORD's people were prophets and that the LORD would put His Spirit upon them!" (Numbers 11:29). When his own sister and brother rejected him, he demonstrated such a meek attitude that the Holy Spirit added an editorial comment, "Now the man Moses was very humble, more than all men who were on the face of the earth" (12:3). When confronted with Israel's rejection of its golden opportunity to enter the promised land from Kadesh-Barnea, Moses again interceded for Israel on the basis of God's loyal love, urgently petitioning the Lord to forgive the rebellious nation (14:13–19).

Two Valleys

However, Scripture does not whitewash any of God's servants, and Moses is no exception. Significantly, two of Moses' major valleys or failures occurred later in life, after most people would assume that he had learned all the lessons he needed to ensure continued stability and a successful finish, including retirement in the promised land. Note also that both of these major failures occurred following significant victories, a risk we face today.

In Numbers 10 the Israelites ended their climactic stay at Mt. Sinai and began moving toward the land of promise. For twelve months Moses had been in constant contact with the Lord—a contact reflected in his optimistic prayer, "Rise up, O LORD! Let Your enemies be scattered, And let those who hate You flee before You" (10:35). Then just three days after Sinai, Israel began murmuring and complaining again—a situation almost identical to what happened three days after the triumph at the Red Sea (Exodus 15). The murmuring of the Israelites prompted a manifestation of judgment: God's anger burned toward the Israelites, some of whom were killed by fire. Yet the Israelites persisted in complaining, especially about their diet. Despite the fact that God had provided them a nourishing food called manna, they chose to focus on what they didn't have. Their diet wasn't varied enough to suit them. So it wasn't as though they were without food or water, as they had been before. They simply had no beef, no lamb, none of the seafood they ate in Egypt; none of the vegetables, the fruits, the spices (Numbers 11:4, 5). In short, they griped that their diet was just too boring.

Now place yourself in Moses' sandals. You've been doing all you can to lead these people. You've delivered God's message to them. You've interceded for them when the Lord was prepared to strike them dead. Now here they are again venting their anger and frustration on you.

Undoubtedly, most of us would respond as Moses did. He became very displeased and depressed. He began focusing his attention inward; and in Numbers 11:11–12, he complains to God, "Why have you afflicted your servant . . . [and] laid the burden of all these people on me?"

Moses' despair reached a climax in verse 15, when he rashly prayed, "If you treat me like this, please kill me here and now . . . and do not let me see my wretchedness!" Without question he had become deeply troubled; he had reached the end of his rope and was prepared to quit.

Have you ever felt that kind of despair? You were ready to throw in the towel; you just couldn't cope with the pressures anymore; something that happened was the last straw, the one that fractured the camel's back.

But amazingly, even though Moses had forgotten God's promises, overlooked God's power, and abandoned God's plan, the Lord didn't reject him. His response to the patriarch's failure was both gracious toward him and enlightening to us. First, God provided seventy elders from among the people to help Moses get the job done (Numbers 11:16). Second, the Lord dealt with the rebellious Israelites who provided the source of much of Moses' irritation. As the Scripture would later put it, "He gave them their request, / But sent leanness into their soul" (Psalm 106:15). In fact, many of the rebels became severely ill as they were eating (Numbers 11:31–33).

Of course, Moses wasn't the only one of God's servants to become so depressed that he felt like dying. Centuries later Elijah would find himself in the same boat, as would David, Jeremiah, and Jonah.

We think the lesson for today is clear. If we don't continue to cling to God's promises, if we don't see his purposeful hand at work in our lives, and if we don't allow others to provide the kind of assistance we need, we too can become stressed out, burned out, and depressed. The good news is that when we reach the end of our rope, God is still there.

A Leadership Explosion

Moses' second major failure occurred in Numbers 20, when the nation returned to Kadesh after forty years of wandering in the wilderness. A new generation was on the scene; and only Moses, Caleb, and Joshua had been present when the Lord had provided water from the rock at Rephidim (Exodus 17). Now the Israelites found themselves in the same situation, without water.

Perhaps the boring routine, the daily grind, had worn Moses down and dulled the edge of his spiritual life. It could have happened to him, and it can happen to us. Perhaps Moses became distracted by grief. After all, his sister, Miriam, had just died. The absence of water prompted the people to contend with Moses and gripe. The patriarch's initial response was right on target. Moses and Aaron went to the door of the tent of meeting and fell on their faces before the Lord. Then for the first time in years, the glory of the Lord appeared—the same Shechinah glory the previous generation had seen at Mount Sinai. God's instructions to Moses were clear: "Take the rod; you and your brother Aaron gather the congregation together. Speak to the rock before their eyes, and it will yield its water" (Numbers 20:8). Moses responded just as we'd expect him to, taking the rod and assembling the nation before the rock.

Then just as things seem to be going according to God's instructions, the leader of the Israelites began improvising. He lashed out in anger, saying, "Hear now, you rebels!" (20:10). Next, for perhaps the only time in his life, Moses elevated himself to the same level as God: "Must we bring water for you out of this rock?" he exploded (20:10). It proved to be an amazing loss of control by a man the Spirit of God had already labeled as the most humble on earth. What a vivid reminder for us! There are two important facts for us to digest from this. First, longevity doesn't ensure ongoing spiritual vitality. Second, each of us is capable of failing, even in our areas of strength. Instead of obeying God and speaking to the rock, Moses struck the rock—not once but twice. Even with his vast experience, his great humility and meekness, and his continued steadfastness under pressure, Moses suffered a major failure in a moment of weakness.

What a lesson for us! Even with all of God's resources, even though we may have an extensive track record of success in serving the Lord, it is still possible to fail—and fail in a major fashion.

You're probably familiar with the consequences of Moses' failure. He would not be permitted to enter the promised land; instead, he was allowed only to view it from Mount Nebo, in the land of the Amalekites. His response to God's discipline demonstrates the maturity and depth of his relationship to the Lord. Instead of being filled with bitterness or self-pity in the aftermath of this final valley, he began focusing his attention on the nation, preparing the Israelites to move into the land, recognizing their need of leadership, and asking God to provide a leader to take his place—a request God answered in the person of Joshua (Numbers 27:16–17).

Three Major Insights

Among the many important insights we can gain from the life of Moses are three major principles. First, though he struggled with how he viewed himself, feeling at times like a failure, Moses was a gifted individual characterized by great meekness (Numbers 12:3). He illustrates that we need to cultivate a balanced view of ourselves and our position in Christ. To put it as Paul did, we are not to think of ourselves more highly than we ought but to realistically assess our abilities based on our position in Christ (Romans 12:3).

Second, Moses was a man marked by faithfulness and steadfastness. In Numbers 12:7 God described him as a faithful man. Many people today are gifted, but few are consistently faithful in using their gifts to the extent Moses did. What made him great in God's sight was not his giftedness as much as his faithfulness as a steward of the many abilities God had entrusted to him.

Finally, the ultimate test of Moses' life and its impact was his face-to-face relationship with God. Deuteronomy 34:10, the inspired postscript to the five biblical books Moses authored, probably written by his close friend Joshua, records: "But since then there has not arisen in Israel a prophet like Moses, whom the Lord knew face to face." To that distinctive description, the author of Hebrews (11:27) adds the fact that Moses "endured as seeing Him who is invisible." For Moses, as for each of us today, a daily walk with the invisible God is the ultimate mark of success, no matter how many peaks and valleys we may encounter and no matter what role we play in life. Whether we lead a nation, shepherd a church, guide a family, or simply follow the Lord and serve him, that vital personal relationship is of utmost importance.

🌿 Moses 🌿

Take-Away Messages from the Past

1. A face-to-face walk with God, cultivated on a daily basis, is of vital importance.

2. The greatest challenges, obstacles, and sources of discouragement often occur after some of the greatest moments of success.

3. God can use even those extended desert periods to build character and to prepare us for the challenges ahead.

4. We need to prepare ourselves and our children early to make the decision to serve and follow the Lord and give him first place in our lives.

5. It's important not to lose sight of the heritage of a godly upbringing even if we experience great success in life.

Choices for Today

1. What are some specific ways you could cultivate an awareness of God's presence in your life, even during your busy routine? One suggestion might involve engaging in brief conversational prayers; another might be repeating verses of Scripture you've memorized.

2. In what ways can you remain alert to the potential for discouragement and even bad decisions following moments of victory and wise choices? (Hint: Read 1 Corinthians 10:12, 13.)

3. What is one specific way you could, if you find yourself in a valley of discouragement, choose to allow God to bring you out of it through his Word, his people, and his provision? (Hint: Check what David did in 1 Samuel 30:6.)

4. What is one specific way you can either choose for yourself or help your children choose to "present your body a living sacrifice, holy, acceptable to God" (Romans 12:1)? After all, it's your reasonable service.

5. Why not choose to thank God each day for the heritage and factors in your life that drew you to him and prepared you for serving him?

Chapter Four

Caleb

How to Finish Well

When it comes to finishing well, few racers of any era could be considered in a league with Eric Liddell, who won an Olympic gold medal in Paris in 1924, then spent the final years of his life in missionary service in China. Who can forget the film about him, *Chariots of Fire*, and his penetrating words of commitment to Christ, "When I run I feel His pleasure."[1]

Early in his career, while running a race, Liddell stumbled and fell. Things looked hopeless at that point. But he picked himself up, resumed the race, thrust his head back in the unorthodox style for which he would become famous, overtook his competitors, and won!

The older we get, the further down life's track, the more finishing well matters to us. The question is: What does it mean to finish well? Scripture gives us several clues. First, we need to be gaining an increased level of wisdom as time goes along. In Psalm 90:12 Moses prayed, "So teach us to number our days, that we may gain a heart of wisdom." A second necessity for finishing well involves continued and increasing fruitfulness. As the psalmist pointed out in Psalm 92:13–15, "Those who are planted in the house of the LORD shall flourish in the courts of our God. They shall still bear fruit in old age. They shall be fresh and flourishing to declare that the LORD is upright." A continued vital relationship with God, a freshness of attitude toward life, a vitality and vigor, and effective service to the Lord that bears fruit for God's glory are all important. A third essential for finishing well can be found in Solomon's statement in

Proverbs 16:31 that the "silver haired head [is] a crown of glory, if it is found in the way of righteousness." Only those who live by God's righteous standards as spelled out in his Word will finish well. Finally, finishing well involves leaving a legacy for the generations that follow, as David noted in Psalm 71:17, 18: "O God, you have taught me from my youth; and to this day I declare your wondrous works. Now also when I'm old and gray headed, O God, do not forsake me, until I declare your strength to this generation, your power to everyone who is to come."

No one was more concerned with finishing well than the Apostle Paul. Writing to the Corinthians (1 Corinthians 9:24–27), whose struggles were numerous and varied, he pointed out: "Do you not know that those who run in a race all run, but one receives the prize? Run in such a way that you may obtain it. And everyone who competes for the prize is temperate in all things. Now they do it to obtain a perishable crown, but we for an imperishable crown. Therefore I run thus: not with uncertainty. Thus I fight, not as one who beats the air. But I discipline my body and bring it into subjection, lest, when I have preached to others, I myself should become disqualified."

A book by John Gilmore, entitled *Ambushed at Sunset: Coping with Mature Adult Temptations*, accurately reflects the reality and wide range of temptations—moral, personal, and interpersonal— that stand in the way of our finishing well. Among the temptations Dr. Gilmore identified as common to those over fifty include the temptation to be bossy, to live in the past, to complain, to gossip, to worry, to procrastinate, and even to be bullheaded.[2] These are all temptations that Caleb managed to avoid. We also would do well to avoid them during our sunset years.

Caleb: The Role Model

Few people of any era finished as well as did Caleb. By the time of his last appearance in Scripture, he was an octogenarian. Yet at a point when most people would be looking for the nearest rocking chair, this incredible individual begs his old friend Joshua for the opportunity to fulfill a decades-long ambition and conquer the high country around Hebron. As respected Bible teacher Warren Wiersbe once pointed out, "If Caleb had been like some senior saints he would have sat down and pouted because the nation wasted forty years of his life, years when he could have been enjoying his inheritance or he could have asked for an easy inheritance, perhaps a quiet valley with a rippling brook. But he asked for a mountain! And no ordinary mountain, for the giants were in control and Caleb would have to defeat them before he could claim his land."[3] Let's consider how this man came to be the epitome of one who remains fruitful and flourishing at midlife and beyond, one who exemplifies the statement of the psalmist: "Those who are planted in the house of the LORD shall flourish in the courts of our God. They shall still bear fruit in old age. They shall be fresh and flourishing" (Psalm 92:13, 14).

Three significant factors contributed to Caleb's incredibly strong finish. As we consider them, we can learn lessons that will help us finish well.

An Optimistic Faith

Caleb's first quality, one that appears early in his record, is optimistic faith. When Caleb first appeared on the scene in Numbers 13, he was about forty years old. Moses had just led the Israelites out of Egypt, through the wilderness where they received the Law at Mt. Sinai, and to a location just south of the promised land in what was called the Wilderness of Paran. At this point twelve men played a role of critical importance: Moses selected them as spies to explore the land of Canaan. They included Caleb and Joshua. Their assignment was to assess the conditions in the land, including the strength and number of its inhabitants, the quality of the agricultural produce and the status of the cities. The report of all the spies referred to the land as possessing great abundance; "it truly flows with milk and honey" (13:27). However, ten of the twelve spies brought back a negative report, concluding "We are not able to go up against the people, for they are stronger than we" (v. 31). Perhaps their best-known sound bite was "we were like grasshoppers in our own sight, and so we were in their sight" (v. 33). These were the men who prompted the Israelites to weep all night and murmur against Moses, Aaron, and the Lord before deciding to select a leader and return to Egypt.

Against this backdrop we see Caleb displaying an incredibly strong faith, which manifested itself in two ways. First, Caleb demonstrated the courage to stand alone. When the twelve spies brought back their initial report, they told Moses, "We went to the land where you sent us. It truly flows with milk and honey" (v. 27). They even presented a cluster of grapes that was so large that two men had to carry it on a pole. "Nevertheless," they continued, "the people who dwell in the land are strong; the cities are fortified and very large; moreover we saw the descendants of Anak there" (v. 28). This negative report continued the chronicle of people who lived in the land, potential foes such as the Amalekites, the Hittites, the Jebusites, the Amorites, and the Canaanites. About the only group they didn't mention were the termites!

As we read this negative report, we can almost feel the mood of the Israelites shifting from one of optimism to gloom. Then suddenly, we read, "Caleb quieted the people before Moses, and said, 'Let us go up at once and take possession, for we are well able to overcome it'" (v. 30). These words are like a ray of light shining into a dark room. Before Moses could speak up to counter the negative reports, even before Joshua joined in, Caleb spoke up, demonstrating the heart, conviction, and courage to stand alone. Later Joshua and Caleb spoke in concert to remind the people, "If the LORD delights in us, then He will bring us into this land and give it to us" (14:8).

Most of us have experienced the paralyzing effect of fear. Perhaps we have sat in a church business meeting where the tide begins to turn against godly leadership, with some individuals making statements in order to undermine confidence and perhaps to distort the facts. We knew we ought to stand up and speak out. But we felt ourselves glued to the pew.

Or maybe we were sitting in a group of colleagues at lunch, discussing a new initiative at work. First, one person and then another chimed in with negative observations. We knew we ought to speak out, but we didn't want to be the first to counter the prevailing mood.

Throughout Scripture we find examples of individuals who demonstrated the courage to stand alone; Daniel, who purposed in his heart not to defile himself with the king's delicacies (Daniel 1:8); Jeremiah, who stood alone to speak the words God put in his mouth against a godless generation in Israel (Jeremiah 1:9); and even Peter, when asked his opinion of Jesus, who said, "You are the Christ, the Son of the living God" (Matthew 16:16). Courage to stand alone is rare, yet it's a quality desperately needed among God's people.

The second way in which Caleb's faith manifested itself was his optimism to look beyond the obstacles. Let's revisit his interaction with the ten spies as they gave their "majority report." Note the contrast: each side had observed the same potential and noted the same obstacles. Compare Caleb's perspective "We are well able to overcome it" (Numbers 13:30) with that of the ten spies: "We are not able to go up against the people, for they are stronger than we" (v. 31). They even used a couple of g-words to generate fear on the part of their audience: "We saw giants . . . we were like grasshoppers" (v. 33).

But Caleb would have no part in their negativity. He heard the murmuring and saw the rebellious intent of his fellow Israelites. Caleb and Joshua tore their clothes in an outward response of grief and intense appeal to the Israelites. "The land we passed through to spy out is an exceedingly good land," they begin (14:7). Reminding the people that God had brought them this far, they urged, "If the LORD delights in us, he will bring us into this land and give it to us. . . . Only, do not rebel against the LORD nor fear the people of the LORD, for they are our bread" (14:8–9). To use our terminology today—they're toast!

How easy it is when circumstances seem to be going against us to become cynical, pessimistic, and fearful. We focus on the obstacles rather than the opportunities. However, if we are to move beyond those obstacles and finish well, we need to have the optimism of a

Caleb, who wound up his appeal by reminding the Israelites, "The LORD is with us. Do not fear them" (14:9). We can take courage and cultivate optimism in the truth that Jesus promised to be with us always, even until the end of the age (Matthew 28:20). And as Paul concluded in Romans 8:31: "If God is for us, who can be against us?"

Perhaps this would be a good time to evaluate your own frame of mind. Whatever age you may be, the question is this: Have you cultivated that optimistic faith, that absolute dependence on God, that can give you the courage to stand alone? Do you have that God-given optimism to look beyond the obstacles and see the potential of what God has in store for you? Perhaps this would be a great time to get alone with the Lord and ask him to renew your courage, to turn your negative mind-set into one of positive, godly optimism, the kind that Caleb demonstrated.

Humble Persistence

The second factor that enabled Caleb to finish so strongly was his humble persistence over decades. Now this wasn't an ingredient that manifested itself at some dramatic point in Caleb's life. Instead, it was a quality God built into his day-to-day experience. In fact, God wants to build a humble persistence into each of our lives. In a radio interview, Dr. George Sweeting, former president of Moody Bible Institute, speaking about his book *Too Soon to Quit*, explained that of the many qualities that are useful for the Christian who wants to finish well, perhaps none is of greater importance than simple persistence.[4] It is a quality the Lord Jesus desired to see in the lives of his followers, as evidenced by the parable he spoke in Luke (18:1): "Men always ought to pray and not lose heart." He never wants us to throw in the towel, quit, or give up. The unified call of Scripture is to constant persistence.

We find major evidence of Caleb's humble persistence in his response to what took place in Numbers 27. Decades had passed since he and Joshua had confronted the other ten spies at Kadesh Barnea. The Lord had warned Moses that he would not be able to go into the land because he struck the rock in the waters of Meribah in the Wilderness of Zin (27:12–14). In response, the old patriarch asked the Lord to guide the Israelites in the appointment of a leader to take Moses' place.

If we were to survey the potential candidates for Moses' successor, two résumés would probably come to the surface early in our search: those of Caleb and Joshua. In fact, we could make a compelling case for Caleb. After all, he spoke first. He stood alone even before Joshua at Kadesh.

Yet the Lord told Moses, "Take Joshua the son of Nun with you, a man in whom is the Spirit, and lay your hand on him; set him before Eleazar the priest and before all the congregation, and inaugurate him in their sight. And you shall give some of your authority to him, that all the congregation of the children of Israel may be obedient" (Numbers 27:18–20).

So how do you suppose Caleb responded to this? Had we had found ourselves in Caleb's sandals, we might have resented the choice of Joshua. We might have withdrawn in silent irritation or perhaps caused a scene. After all, these are common ways people respond to disappointment today. Perhaps we have even responded to some major disappointment in this way, when another person received the promotion we deserved or someone who hadn't demonstrated the longevity or support we had was appointed to the church board.

However, Scripture records absolutely no resentment on Caleb's part, not a word of complaining, not even a pout. In fact, the passage doesn't even mention Caleb, and this implies—as do Moses' commendation of Caleb (Numbers 32:12) and Caleb's appearance before Joshua to request the rights to claim Hebron (Joshua 14:6)—that this man had not a molecule of resentment in his body.

How easy it is for us to succumb to the temptation to feel resentment toward others, until our bitterness and unresolved anger eat away at our insides like an emotional cancer. Resentment prevents many of God's choice servants from finishing well. May we follow Caleb's example and say no to the temptation.

Moses memorialized Caleb's humble persistence during the decades between Kadesh Barnea and the conquest of Canaan in a statement he made to the members of the tribes of Reuben and Gad when they asked to be allowed to settle on the east side of the Jordan. Moses' response to their request was quick and pointed: "Shall your brethren go to war while you sit here? Now why will you discourage the heart of the children of Israel?" (Numbers 32:6, 7). Reminding them of how the ten spies discouraged the hearts of the Israelites at Kadesh and how angry the Lord was at the entire generation because it failed to wholly follow the Lord, Moses pointed out two notable exceptions.

"Except Caleb the son of Jephunneh, the Kenizzite, and Joshua the son of Nun, for they have wholly followed the LORD" (32:12). Almost as an aside, Moses set the record straight about Caleb and Joshua. In doing so he reminded these Israelites that Caleb was not a pure Israelite by birth. His father had been a Kenizzite, a member of another nation. Caleb's commitment to the Lord God of Israel was clear and unwavering. He, like Joshua, followed the Lord with all his heart, which brings us to the third and final factor that helped Caleb finish so strongly.

A Total Commitment to God and His Purpose

The scene now shifts to the promised land. Joshua had led the Israelites across the Jordan River, and they had conquered much of the land. The descendants of Judah, led by Caleb, approached the aging Joshua at Gilgal. At a time when we might expect Caleb to take it easy, the word *retirement* just wasn't in his vocabulary, nor was the word *quit*. Caleb had just one speed—all out for God—as he asked Moses for permission to capture Hebron, the part of the land of which he had dreamed for years (Joshua 14:6–14). Even at his advanced age, he showed total commitment to God and God's purpose.

How did Caleb demonstrate this kind of commitment? For one thing he exhibited a keen mind for God's promises. Though he was eighty-five, he remembered clearly the time when Moses sent him at age forty to spy out the land, "And I brought back word to him as it was in my heart" (Joshua 14:7). According to Caleb, the other spies "made the heart of the people melt, but I wholly followed the LORD my God" (v. 8). The old traveler recalled the promise Moses made on that long-ago day: "Surely the land where your foot has trodden shall be your inheritance and your children's forever, because you have wholly followed the LORD my God" (v. 9). He remembered God's promises, and he maintained his focus on them through the years.

One of the most important keys to our finishing life well today is to maintain a keen mind for the promises of God's Word. Can we trust God's promises today? The answer is an unequivocal yes, as Paul noted in 2 Corinthians 1:20: "For all the promises of God in Him are Yes, and in Him Amen, to the glory of God through us." Throughout his Word God has promised his presence, his provision, his encouragement, and his peace. Perhaps no single factor is of greater importance than to make God's Word an integral part of our lives. We do so by reading and studying it regularly, learning what it says, understanding what it means, and applying its timeless principles to our experience today (see Nehemiah 8:8).

When Don Hawkins was growing up, he was involved in two important Scripture memory programs—Children's Bible Mission and Bible Memory Association. Each program required him to memorize hundreds of Bible verses. Many decades later those verses still play a key role in his own walk with the Lord and ministry to others. Frank Minirth and Roy Vogel have also given themselves to memorizing Scripture, and they can directly attribute the impact of their respective ministries to their commitment to the Word of God. If you have not made God's promises and God's Word an important part of your life, you are putting yourself in direct risk of not finishing well. It's never too late to start reading, studying, and memorizing God's holy Word.

Another way Caleb showed his total commitment to God and his purpose was by expressing a spirit of thankfulness for God's care.

"And now, behold, the LORD has kept me alive, as He said these forty-five years," he said to Moses (Joshua 14:10). No, Caleb didn't have the attitude that says "I've done all the right things, taken care of myself, maintained my physical fitness." Nor did he think, *I'm just a lucky guy. Things have worked out well for me.* He clearly saw the hand of God at work in his life and didn't hesitate to give God the credit.

In a day when people feel entitled to the good things of life and often relate well-being and prosperity to random chance or luck, it's of vital importance that we cultivate a spirit of thankfulness to God for his care in our lives. The psalmist wrote, "Bless the LORD, O my soul, and forget not all His benefits" (Psalm 103:2). Years ago a good friend challenged Don to keep a record of at least one thing for which he could be thankful every day, one piece of evidence of God's providential hand in his life. He has endeavored to do so since.

Caleb also demonstrated his total commitment to God with a physical vigor to pursue God's plan. "Here I am this day, eighty-five years old," he remarked. "As yet I'm as strong this day as on the day that Moses sent me; just as my strength was then, so now is my strength . . . for going out and for coming in" (Joshua 14:10, 11). The remarkable evidence of this man's robust vitality was that he considered himself as strong at eighty-five as he had been at forty.

Part of the reason for Caleb's physical vigor was the number of miles he had walked through the wilderness with the Israelites, not to mention the miles he covered spying out the land of Canaan. Physical exercise is important for well-being in every area—physical, emotional, and even spiritual. The older we get, the easier it is to become a couch potato. After all, we don't have the "advantage" Caleb had of having to cover virtually every mile on foot! Yet it's important that we recognize the fact that God wants us to take steps to maintain our physical health. That's why Paul reminded young Timothy of the benefits of bodily exercise (1 Timothy 4:8). As the apostle pointed out in 1 Corinthians 6:19, the body is the temple of the Holy Spirit—and we need to care for it in order to maintain physical vigor so that we can finish well.

Caleb's total commitment to God and God's purpose was apparent in the emotional courage he demonstrated to challenge God's foes. Even though there were pagan giants, Anakim, in the fortified cities of the hill country, he was convinced that God would be with him and that he would be able to drive them out, based on the Lord's promises (Numbers 14:12). So many times we find ourselves paralyzed by a variety of fears—fear of the future, fear of the unknown, fear of intimidating people and circumstances. Yet as Paul told Timothy, "God has not given us a spirit of fear, but of power and of love and of a sound mind" (2 Timothy 1:7). Fear can be particularly paralyzing as we reach our older years; yet the promise of God's presence, protection, and provision can continue to sustain us, no matter what we face.

For many years Don's friend Jim feared the prospect of cancer. His father and an uncle died of prostate cancer, and he said, "I just knew I was going to get it sometime." He wasn't able to conquer that fear until he was actually diagnosed with cancer himself. Spending time with his pastor and several good friends enabled Jim to cultivate the courage to face his malignancy, secure the treatment he needed, and cultivate the kind of positive fear-free attitude that enabled him to keep going well beyond what could have been a debilitating halt to his effective ministry.

The ultimate essence of Caleb's total commitment to God and God's purpose is reflected in a descriptive phrase about him that appears several times in Scripture: "He wholly followed the LORD" (Joshua 14:14). Caleb's commitment to the God of Israel was not half-hearted, not timid, not based on circumstances. It was the commitment to which Jesus spoke when he underscored the importance of the first of all the commandments: "And you shall love the LORD your God with all your heart, with all your soul, with all your mind, and with all your strength. This is the first commandment" (Mark 12:30). A wholehearted love for God—as opposed to a half-hearted, timid commitment to the Lord—is of vital importance in our finishing well. Caleb used this phrase to describe his own commitment in Joshua 14:8: "I wholly followed the LORD my God." Moses used it in Joshua 14:8, 9: "Because you have wholly followed the LORD my God," as well as in his description of Caleb and Joshua in Numbers 32:12. Most important of all, the Lord used this phrase to describe Caleb in his response to Moses in Numbers 14:24: "But My servant Caleb, because he has a different spirit in him and has followed Me fully, I will bring into the land where he went, and his descendants shall inherit it." That was Caleb's letter of reference from the Lord, and it came to be the promise upon which he based his later exploits of faith.

One more thing about Caleb's effort to finish well: he left a legacy of faith and persistence for future generations. We can see this in the commitment to God and the cause of Israel of his daughter Achsah and his son-in-law Othniel, who later became one of the judges of Israel (Joshua 15:18, 19).

So how can we finish well? We can follow the example of Caleb, who demonstrated an optimistic faith in midlife that included the courage to stand alone as well as the optimism to look beyond daunting obstacles. We can cultivate a humble persistence for decades, refusing to allow resentment or discouragement to get in the way. And we can cultivate a total commitment to God and his purpose in our lives. We can do this by exhibiting a keen mind for God's promises as found in his Word; a spirit of thankfulness for his care; physical vigor to pursue his plan for our lives; the emotional courage to challenge obstacles and foes; and most of all, the spiritual commitment to follow the Lord faithfully.

The Bible does not tell us where Caleb was buried. In fact, in his final appearance in Scripture, he was organizing his troops, including his family, to drive out more enemy troops and to occupy more territory for the Lord (Joshua 15:13–19). Perhaps someday an archeologist will find near Hebron the tomb of this great old warrior. If so, the epitaph will surely read, "He wholly followed the Lord his God."

May it be said of us at the end of our lives as well.

🌿 Caleb 🌿

Take-Away Messages from the Past

1. We don't have to be in the majority to take a stand for God. We just need the courage to stand alone.

2. Unlike the ten spies who gave the negative majority report and then disappeared into obscurity, Caleb and Joshua stood for what was right; and their faith became legendary.

3. Caleb looked at the same circumstances that discouraged the spies and saw potential for victory through God.

4. Fear can lead to rebellion against God, especially when it causes us to refuse to follow his leading in our lives (Numbers 14:9).

5. It is appropriate to feel grief when others rebel against God and reject his power, provision, and purpose (see Numbers 14:6).

6. Caleb never minimized the obstacles or pretended things would be easy; he simply looked beyond the obstacles to the provision of God.

7. Caleb continued to cooperate with Joshua and respect his leadership even after Joshua was selected to lead the Israelites, a role that Caleb could have sought.

8. Down through the years, Caleb continued to remember and rehearse in his mind God's promise to give him the land he had scouted out when he was forty.

9. Caleb received the inheritance God had promised, Hebron, because of his total commitment to following the Lord God of Israel (Joshua 14:14).

10. Caleb apparently communicated his positive faith and optimistic values to his family, as his daughter's attitude demonstrates (Joshua 15:18, 19).

Choices for Today

1. What specific choice can you make to move toward following the Lord with all your heart?

2. What specific choice can you make to move toward walking with the Lord more closely to become more like him?

3. What specific choice can you make to move toward realizing that even though the obstacles may be large, it's always too soon to give up?

4. What specific choice can you make to move toward realizing that at times you may be in the minority, even called on to stand alone, but that to do so is ultimately worth it?

5. What specific choice can you make to move toward realizing that God is big enough to handle even your biggest challenge?

6. What specific choice can you make to help you realize that the real issue is not the size of the obstacle without but the size of the heart within?

7. What specific choice can you make to help you avoid expecting things to always get easier and instead realizing that obstacles of some kind will always exist?

8. What specific choice can you make to allow the Word of God to help you make it through the long haul, through the daily grind?

9. What specific choice can you make to make finishing well a top priority?

10. What specific choice can you make to move toward taking care of your whole being—physical, mental, emotional, and spiritual? (See 1 Thessalonians 5:23.)

Chapter Five

Naomi

Battling Adversity and Bitterness

What would you consider to be the number-one mental health problem in the United States today? If you took a clipboard and surveyed a dozen people at a modern suburban shopping mall, you'd likely get a variety of answers. Clinical depression would probably rank first, perhaps followed by bipolar or manic-depressive disorder, panic attacks or other anxiety disorders, schizophrenia, or even attention deficit disorder with hyperactivity.

Some time ago two of this book's authors were having dinner with Dr. Joe Stowell, president of Moody Bible Institute. Following dinner, one of us asked Dr. Stowell, "What do you consider to be America's greatest mental health problem?"

After a brief pause, Dr. Stowell responded with conviction, "I'm convinced that bitterness is the number-one problem we see in the lives of individuals that affects their mental health."

Frankly, the authors of this book couldn't agree more. Bitterness—the toxic result of unresolved anger over the hurts, griefs, and plights of life—probably affects more of us than we'd ever admit. It plays a major role in the interpersonal conflicts as well as emotional struggles so many of us face.

How Bitterness Develops

So how does bitterness get to be such a big problem? Possibly because of its insidious nature. Like termites working on a house, bitterness eats away in silence, causing great damage over time. Frequently we allow it to do so, justifying our feelings on the basis of the fact that life hasn't treated us fairly or that someone has done us an injustice. And sometimes our feelings are right. Frankly, we all suffer more hurts at the hands of others than we'd like to in this fallen world. But being hurt doesn't have to lead directly to being bitter. Unfortunately, all too often it does.

The first step in assessing the anatomy of bitterness, in understanding how bitterness works, is acknowledging that we have suffered a wound of some kind. Such a wound could involve physical pain; more frequently it is emotional. Perhaps someone begins spreading gossip about us, true or untrue. Maybe we're insulted or slighted, omitted from the guest list at a dinner party or the nomination list for church leadership.

That leads to the second step in the emotional chain reaction that leads to bitterness: we become angry. It's important to understand that anger is not always a sin. We know this to be true from Paul's words in Ephesians 4:26, 27: "Be angry, and do not sin: do not let the sun go down on your wrath, nor give place to the devil." The literal meaning of Paul's words from the original Greek text is this: become angry—that is, face your anger honestly. In verse 25 Paul had just underscored the value of "speaking truth" (Don's translation). If we are to be honest with each other, we need to be honest with ourselves about anger.

The problem is that many of us are good at denying our anger. After all, nice Christian people don't get angry. Have you ever heard that one? The fact is that nice Christian people—even mature, godly people—do become angry.

So how do we become angry without sinning? Paul responds, "Do not let the sun go down on your wrath" (Ephesians 4:26). In other words, resolve anger—whether toward people, ourselves, or toward God—before bedtime. You see, unlike today when so many of us stay up to watch the news and maybe our favorite late show, in biblical times when the sun went down, people commonly went to bed. And how often are we tempted to carry anger over from day to day, week to week, month to month, even year to year? The results can be devastating.

Marjorie and her sister, Jackie, had been the best of friends ever since childhood. They and their husbands had vacationed together; they spent time together caring for their aging mothers; and they talked on the phone at least once every day. Then one day, when Marjorie was hospitalized, Jackie didn't visit her. Even though she found out later that Jackie had been ill, Marjorie felt slighted. Over time the sense of hurt and anger continued to fester and develop. Before long, misunderstandings fueled the rift, and Marjorie broke off all contact with the sister with whom she had been so close.

Four years passed before the two sisters experienced a meaningful breakthrough in their relationship, four years that Marjorie later admitted were "the worst years of my life. I was so bitter and so angry toward my sister I imagined things she had said toward me, things she was doing to hurt me. If only I had chosen to forgive her for the one or two small things she had done. Bitterness wasted precious years of our lives."

How many of us have experienced that kind of loss, simply because we refused to let go of anger and let the sun set on our wrath?

Her Name Means "Pleasant"

Perhaps no one in Scripture had more bitterness to overcome, more anger-producing adversity, than Naomi. Her name means "pleasant," but for Naomi life had become extremely bitter. We usually think of Naomi as a mother-in-law and only consider her in the context of her well-known daughter-in-law, Ruth, one of only two women for whom books in Scripture were named (the other is Esther). Yet Naomi provides us with a classic lesson about how women and men of all ages and all walks of life can become bitter. Her story also provides us with a road map for recovery from bitterness. Naomi, a woman just like us, struggled with the hurts and pains and losses of life. Over time God helped her recover. To understand her troubled experience of bitterness, we must first consider her circumstances and the way she responded to them, then take a look at her road map to recovery.

Responses Lead to Bitterness

As we read the account of what happened to Elimelech and his wife, Naomi, in the beginning of the book of Ruth, we might conclude that Naomi's circumstances led to her bitterness. After all, Naomi went through one of the most stressful series of events any person of any time might have experienced. She lived in a troubled period in Israel, when the judges ruled. Life in that godless time was lived under the mantra "everyone did what was right in his own eyes" (Judges 21:25). Sounds a little like life in the twenty-first century, doesn't it?

Against this backdrop a famine occurred. Now most of us in affluent North America have never experienced anything quite like a famine. The closest most of us have come to such an experience might be the massive power blackout that affected nine states and two Canadian provinces for two days during August 2003, the devastation of hurricanes such as Andrew in south Florida in 1992, or the killer fires of southern California in November 2003. But those tragedies don't really compare with month after month with no rain, crops drying up, and no food available. Several countries in North Africa have recently experienced famines in which thousands of people have died, and in which children are regularly affected by malnutrition and starvation. That's how things were in Israel.

As a result, two residents of Bethlehem (the name literally means "house of bread" in Hebrew) decided to leave home and move outside the land of Israel to Moab. There's something joltingly wrong in this decision, and we see just how wrong it is when we realize that the name of one of them, Elimelech, literally means "my God is king." The Lord God, Israel's Ruler and Benefactor, had promised to provide for his people in their land of promise, Israel. He had also warned them to have no contact with the Moabites, persistent enemies of Israel. Perhaps you recall that the Moabite people were named for the son that Lot had from an incestuous relationship with his eldest daughter (Genesis 19:37). The Moabites lived in the southeast of Judah and east of the Dead Sea, in a barren land that was not nearly as fertile as the land of promise where Elimelech and Naomi lived. But for some reason, Elimelech and Naomi decided to move there, even though God had specifically ruled out Moab as part of the land of promise (Deuteronomy 2:9). Further, God had instructed that no Moabite was to enter the Lord's congregation, even to the tenth generation, because they had not treated the Israelites hospitably during Israel's trek from Egypt to the promised land (23:3, 4). So here was a family struggling with a famine and for some reason deciding to move to Moab and settle there (Ruth 1:2). Frequently our bitterness results from decisions we make that leave us outside the will of God, separated from the place and circumstances where God wants to bless us, and frequently because we simply cannot and will not trust God to care for our needs.

Following this decision to move came a devastating series of losses. First, Naomi's husband died. Moving the fifty miles from Bethlehem to Moab had undoubtedly been stressful—most of us can vividly recall the stresses we experienced while moving! And speaking of stress, Naomi experienced the death of a spouse—the highest cause of stress on the modern Holmes-Rahe stress scale[1] (Ruth 1:3).

Next, Naomi experienced the empty nest—another modern stressor—as her two sons married wives from Moab (these mixed-race marriages were probably stressful in themselves, particularly because they violated the biblical injunction of accepting Moabites into the covenant community of Israel). Then both sons, Mahlon and Chilion, died within a short time (Ruth 1:5). Their names meant "weak" and "wasting," perhaps indicating they weren't in the best of health. And to top it all off, neither son had produced a child who might care for Naomi in her old age. So here she was, abandoned, left by her husband in a foreign land, struggling with a series of devastating losses. Before long she decided to make a second major move and return to Israel, because she had heard that Jehovah had visited his people and given them bread (Ruth 1:6).

If we assign numerical values based on the Holmes-Rahe stress scale (this stress chart can be found in Chapter Eleven) to all the stressors in Naomi's life, we can calculate that Naomi had experienced over five hundred stress points, about three times the stress threshold that places many modern people at risk for serious physical and emotional illness.

But we can't help noticing another major factor in Naomi's life—debilitating bitterness. As she prepared to return to Israel, she urged her daughters-in-law not to go with her: "Are there still sons in my womb, that they may be your husbands? . . . for I am too old to have a husband. If I should say I have hope, if I should have a husband tonight, and should also [conceive and] bear sons, would you wait for them till they were grown?" (1:11–13). Naomi is hopeless, recognizing that she is past child-bearing age and cannot hope to provide husbands for her daughters-in-law.

But then notice where she lays the blame for her dire circumstances: "No, my daughters; for it grieves me very much for your sakes that the hand of the LORD has gone out against me" (1:13). From Naomi's perspective God had set his face against her. The Lord was to blame for what had happened—or so she thought.

But before we rush to condemn Naomi, let's ask: Do we not sometimes engage in the same kind of thing? Living in a fallen world, making spiritual and other choices that are questionable at best, probably God-defying at worst—just as Elimelech and Naomi had—we then turn around and blame God for the consequences. Even if we didn't make choices that directly caused the calamity in our lives, we frequently lay the results of living in a fallen world at the hand of our perfect Creator, who loves us and always desires what is best for us. How many times do our battles with bitterness result from our tendency to blame God for whatever happens to be wrong in our lives?

Bitter as she had become, Naomi urged her daughters-in-law to go away and leave her. Frequently when we struggle with bitterness, we isolate ourselves from those who might provide us with the encouragement to break through to an attitude of bitter-free hope.

Whereas Naomi's major liability at this point was her bitterness, her strongest asset was her loving, persistent daughter-in-law, Ruth. Whereas Orpah kissed her mother-in-law and returned to Moab, Ruth decided to cling to Naomi. The Hebrew word translated "clung," used in Ruth 1:14, carries the same idea of a lifelong commitment that a wife makes to her husband. When Naomi urged Ruth to follow the example of her sister-in-law, who had returned to her people and her gods—a shocking statement from the one who had expressed faith in the one true God of Israel, although certainly not inconsistent with bitterness—Ruth responded with some of the most poignant words in Scripture: "Entreat me not to leave you, / Or to turn back from following after you; / For wherever you go, I will go, / And wherever you lodge, I will lodge; / Your people shall be my people, and your God, my God. / Where you die, I will die, and there will I be buried. / The LORD do so to me, and more also, / If anything but death parts you and me" (1:16, 17).

This remarkable statement of commitment, frequently used between Christian marriage partners in the recitation of their vows, actually was Ruth's expression of steadfast determination to remain part of her mother-in-law's life. Ultimately, Ruth was to be a source of God's provision for Naomi in her old age.

Bitter in Bethlehem

Even though Naomi had Ruth and was returning to the land of promise and the place of God's provision, she still hadn't overcome her bitterness. When the two women arrived in Bethlehem, the whole town was buzzing. The women said, "Is this Naomi?" (1:19). Perhaps she had aged in appearance or even lost many pounds because of the famine.

However, her response is significant: "Do not call me Naomi; call me Mara, for the Almighty has dealt very bitterly with me" (1:20). In effect, she was saying, "I'm a bitter person. I should be identified as such. Basically, it's God's fault. He has brought this bitterness into my life." This is what she accused God of with four specific charges. But before you judge Naomi for her hard response to God, ask yourself if you've ever done the same.

First, she says, God dealt bitterly with me. He's given me a raw deal in life. Second, he brought me back empty. He wiped out the resources I had. You'll note that Naomi had forgotten the fact that life was pretty empty before she and Elimelech had left for Moab, due to the famine in the land. She had also lost sight of the news she had received in Moab that the Lord had visited his people in Israel to provide for their needs. Third, she says, "The LORD has testified against me" (1:21)—in other words, "God has taken up a legal position as my adversary." How frequently we hear people say, "God's against me; he's turned his back on me," even when he never has. Fourth, she says, "The LORD afflicted me"—in other words, "He really hurt me." But did Naomi consider where the series of hurts she had experienced actually came from? Without question she had been hurt, deeply and in many ways. Let's not minimize the pain she had experienced. However, when she experienced (or we experience) pain, it's important not to lay the blame for it at the feet of a good and loving God.

So here is Naomi, back in her land yet struggling with bitterness, resenting God and his people, withdrawing even from her former friends and neighbors. But she still had Ruth—and God was about to bring a man named Boaz into their lives, and ultimately use the romance of Ruth and Boaz's relationship to help Naomi recover from bitterness.

Naomi's Recovery

Even though the book of Ruth can be accurately called "the romance of redemption,"[2] to a great degree the book centers on Naomi. In fact, three of its four chapters begin with her; only the fourth starts with Boaz.

For our purposes the important thing to note is how Naomi recovered from her bitterness. She took eight significant steps, steps that can help us when we find ourselves in a struggle with bitter feelings.

Step One: Return Home to the Lord

Naomi's recovery actually began while she was still in Moab, when she initiated a return to her homeland. When we find ourselves stuck in bitterness, we often become isolated from God, out of fellowship with his people, and out of God's will for our lives. Naomi apparently came to the realization that she would never experience God's blessing in the land where God had told the Israelites not to live and among the people he told them not to associate with. Even though she felt bitter toward the Lord, she realized he was blessing people in the promised land—and she decided it was time to return home.

Perhaps you've been out of church for years, isolated from God's people, refusing to read God's Word because of something he or one of his children did to you years ago. Consider taking the first step Naomi did. Get back into fellowship with God by confessing your sin, beginning to spend time in his Word every day, and returning to fellowship with the Lord's people in a local church that teaches his Word and provides caring, supportive fellowship. And if you've never taken that initial step of admitting that you are a sinner in need of a savior and trusting Jesus, who died to pay for your sins and arose to prove the validity of that payment, that's the place to begin.

Step Two: Admit Your Bitterness

Naomi moved away from bitterness by admitting she was bitter in Ruth 1:20. By asking to be called Mara, she candidly admitted to being bitter. Often this is the hardest step. We find it so easy to deny our emotions: "I'm not angry, only a bit irritated"; "No, I'm not bitter, of course not, why would I be bitter?" And then we list all the hurtful things that all the hurtful people have done to us.

Just as it's vital for anyone who wants to recover from drug or alcohol addiction to start by admitting he or she is addicted, so the bitter individual must admit to bitterness.

Step Three: Get Close to Someone You Can Trust

Naomi allowed a relationship to develop between herself and Ruth. Even though she had initially done everything she could to push both her daughters-in-law away, she finally responded to Ruth's loving expression of commitment. "When [Naomi] saw that she was determined to go with her, she stopped speaking to her" (1:18). In other words, she quit telling Ruth to go back home. And the two of them journeyed together to Bethlehem.

Whenever we have fallen into the pain of bitterness, we typically withdraw from encouraging relationships. One of the most important things we can do is to open our hearts and lives and allow such a relationship to develop. Perhaps you have been struggling with bitterness, and you realize a daughter-in-law, a brother-in-law, or a friend at church could be the key to help you recover. Don't yield to the temptation to withdraw from that compassionate person. Don't allow spite to keep you isolated. Instead, open yourself up to a loving mutual encouragement. The author of Hebrews (10:24, 25) puts it this way: "And let us consider one another in order to stir up love and good works, not forsaking the assembling of ourselves together, as is the manner of some, but exhorting one another, and so much the more as you see the Day approaching."

Step Four: Work on Adjusting Your Attitude

Naomi began to develop an attitude of optimism. Bitterness and a negative, cynical spirit seem to go hand in hand. But finally, when the two of them returned to Bethlehem and Ruth encountered Boaz as she gleaned in the field, Naomi allowed optimism to reenter her life. Picture the scene: Naomi's sitting at home, waiting for her daughter-in-law to return. *Probably nothing to eat again today,* she might have thought. Then Ruth turned up, carrying an ephah of barley—perhaps as much as thirty pounds. *Not bad*, her mother-in-law must have thought.

We read her divinely recorded response; "And her mother-in-law said to her, 'Where have you gleaned today, and where did you work? Blessed be the one who took notice of you'" (Ruth 2:19). Naomi began with an acknowledgment of the generous hand of God in showing favor toward the two women.

Then she learned the name of the man in whose fields Ruth had gleaned. Suddenly, Naomi became downright positive: "Blessed be he of the LORD who has not forsaken His kindness to the living and the dead!" (2:20). She was saying, in effect, "Boaz is a relative, Ruth, one of our near kinsmen."

How do we develop a positive attitude, a sense of optimism? We simply pause to see God's hand of blessing at work. "God hasn't forsaken us," Naomi affirmed. "He didn't forget the two of us who are still living or our dead husbands. He's sent someone into our lives to meet our needs and make a difference." Although she didn't know exactly how God would use Boaz in their lives, she could already see the Lord's hand at work.

Are there ways in which God has been working in your life, even though you've been blinded by bitterness and unable to see? Take some time to sit down with a pen and paper and write down all the evidence of God's work in your life. Some incidents may be very small; others may be quite large. But the fact is that God cares about you and is demonstrating that in what he does. Remember the words of the psalmist: "Bless the LORD, O my soul; . . . And forget not all His benefits" (Psalm 103:1, 2).

Step Five: Reverse Self-Centeredness

The next two steps in Naomi's journey out of bitterness grew directly out of her budding attitude of optimism. First, she centered herself on others. She began to see God's hand of blessing not only in her life but in Ruth's and to recognize the fact that God was still gracious, even to the extent that he had not abandoned their dead husbands' family. In doing so, she blessed Boaz: "Blessed be he of the LORD!" (Ruth 2:20), she cried out. One of the keys to overcoming bitterness is to break free of the self-centeredness a bitter spirit tends to produce. When we can look around us and see the needs of others, pray for them, and reach out to affirm them and help them in their pain and need, we will have taken an important step in overcoming feelings of bitterness.

Step Six: Cultivate a Spirit of Thankfulness

Out of Naomi's optimism grew her attitude of thankfulness. "The Lord hasn't abandoned us" (2:20) she expressed as she rethought her interpretation of the tragic events that occurred since she and her husband had decided to move from Bethlehem to Moab. No longer did she feel abandoned by the Lord; no longer was her life marked by ungratefulness. Instead, she had begun practicing what the psalmist would later urge, "Be thankful to Him, and bless His name. For the LORD is good; His mercy is everlasting, and His truth endures to all generations" (Psalm 100:4, 5).

If you're not already doing so, begin keeping a journal of all the blessings, small and large, that the Lord brings into your life. Then whenever you feel life dragging you down or you feel tempted to become bitter, you can go back to this book of blessings and remind yourself just how much you have to be thankful for.

Step Seven: Let Others Help You

Naomi took a seventh step in her recovery from bitterness when she allowed herself to be ministered to: "What you're doing is good, my daughter," she said to Ruth (Ruth 2:22). Unlike some bitter individuals who don't want anyone to do anything for them, Naomi recognized the value of opening herself up to Ruth's ministry and allowing her to continue to glean in Boaz's field throughout the harvest season.

One of the keys to overcoming bitterness is to allow others to reach out to us. As Paul told the Thessalonians, we are to "comfort each other and edify one another" (1 Thessalonians 5:11). It's important that each of us reaches out to encourage and minister to others. It's also important that we allow others to minister to us as well.

Step Eight: Reach out to Help Others

Naomi's final step in her journey from bitterness to blessing was taking the initiative on behalf of Ruth. Even though she might ultimately lose her, Naomi said to Ruth, "My daughter, shall I not seek security for you that it may be well with you?" (Ruth 3:1). Don't miss the significance of this seemingly cryptic statement. In essence, what Naomi was saying was, I'm going to work behind the scenes to see if I can help arrange a relationship with Boaz, our kinsman. Then she developed a creative plan for Ruth to present herself privately to Boaz following the celebration that took place when the barley harvest ended.

It's important to note that there was no hint of immorality or impropriety in what Ruth did. Naomi was simply following the custom of her day, using events and circumstances to seek what was best for her daughter-in-law. In doing so, she ultimately experienced the blessing of seeing Ruth happily married, and she reaped a great harvest of blessing herself.

Naomi's Benefits

And just what blessings and benefits did Naomi receive?

At the conclusion of the story, with Boaz and Ruth happily married, we discover that Naomi's family name continued—which had seemed like an impossibility during her bitter days in Moab (4:10).

Naomi also obtained personal and family security, which her new son-in-law, Boaz, would guarantee (4:5).

She obtained the provision of all her needs, and her neighbors prayed, "May you prosper in Ephrathah and be famous in Bethlehem" (4:11).

She ultimately obtained a grandson, which gave tangible evidence of the Lord's continued blessing (4:13, 14). All of us who are grandparents know what a great joy this was to her.

She brought glory to God in the events that took place in her life as her neighbors and friends said to her, "Blessed be the LORD, who has not left you this day without a close relative" (4:14).

Naomi obtained a loving son-in-law who became a restorer and a sustainer of life (4:15).

Finally, Naomi began a new career as grandmother and nurse (4:16).

So what concluding observations can we draw from our examination of Naomi's road to recovery from bitterness? First, Naomi experienced the grace of God, which enabled her to grow old without remaining bitter. Whether you're a man or a woman, why don't you begin asking God to keep you from allowing bitterness to become a dominant characteristic of your final days?

Second, Naomi's grandson was named Obed, which means "servant" in Hebrew. One of the reasons for this is that Naomi herself demonstrated the heart of a servant. One of the keys of overcoming self-centeredness and bitterness is to develop a servant's heart toward others. Naomi became a servant to her daughter-in-law, her son-in-law, and ultimately to her grandson. May we develop that same kind of servant's heart toward others.

Finally, even though Naomi had felt isolated from the plan and hand of God, she and her daughter-in-law became a part of the royal line that led to David, her grandson's grandson. That line ultimately led to Jesus Christ. So Naomi, and even Ruth, who came from the forbidden land of Moab, became living demonstrations of the grace of God and part of God's significant and eternal plan.

And it all happened because Naomi took the appropriate steps to beat bitterness.

🌿 Naomi 🌿

Take-Away Messages from the Past

1. Bad circumstances can happen to any of us, but they don't have to cause us to become bitter. Bitterness is, after all, a choice.

2. The more stresses we have, the more losses we experience, the greater the temptation to become bitter. We need to be aware of that temptation and take steps to counter it.

3. Admitting our bitterness is a major step in overcoming it. We'll never break through as long as we remain in denial.

4. Centering ourselves on others rather than becoming self-centered can provide us with the momentum to overcome bitter feelings that grow out of a sense of woundedness.

5. It is important to cultivate an attitude of thankfulness. Begin by documenting things you are thankful for.

6. The ultimate test of healing from bitterness is when we've come to the place where we can reach out to help someone else without stumbling over our bitter feelings from the past.

Choices for Today

1. Name one specific way you might choose to admit that you're bitter, if you are.

2. Name one specific way you might choose to move back into fellowship with God and into contact with God's people even in the midst of stress in your life.

3. Name one specific way you might choose to develop a spirit of optimism. Read and meditate on Philippians 4:7, 8.

4. Name one specific way you might choose to make others rather than yourself your focus. You'll be amazed how difficult it is to remain bitter when you're focused on those around you.

5. Begin a daily log or journal in which you write down at least one thing for which you are thankful each day; then review it at least weekly.

6. Look for someone you can help or encourage in a tangible way; then do it!

Chapter Six

David

Defeating Life's Giants

"Why is everything in life such a hassle?" Harland's face was etched with frustration as he sat across from his pastor in a coffee shop, his lunch relatively untouched. "I just feel like I'm always at war—in my work, my marriage, even at church. Sometimes I feel like I'm wearing a sign that says, Shoot me."

Harland was the youngest of seven children, and that, coupled with his short stature, seemed to lead to a great deal of conflict throughout his early life.

"It seems like I fought my way through junior high and high school," he continued. "Then after I married Jenny, we seemed to get into it just about every other day. Not physically, you understand. I never laid a hand on her, but we argued like cats and dogs."

Harland went on to explain how he had felt overwhelmed when their firstborn son, Todd, was born. Todd had chronic asthma and required a series of surgeries to fix his cleft palate.

"At work it's been the same. I lost two jobs: one because they downsized me; the other [because] my boss was like Simon Legree—a real tyrant who always seemed to take things out on me for some reason."

"So you felt rejected?" Pastor Mike asked after taking a sip of his iced tea.

"I have," Todd replied, a note of intensity in his voice. "But I think the greatest rejection I have felt has come from my father. I never was good enough to please him; in fact, at times he acted like

I wasn't even on the planet. As for my sister and brother-in-law, they just don't like me or my family." Harland paused, sipped his coffee, and then summarized his feelings, "I guess I just consider myself like David surrounded by Goliaths."

Taking on Giants

We've probably all used the phrase *to take on a giant* when talking about handling obstacles and adversities at work, in our families, or in other areas of life. It's a concept that comes right out of the life of David, who took on and defeated the Philistine champion, Goliath of Gath.

David, who began as a humble shepherd boy, the youngest of eight sons of Jesse of Bethlehem, became one of the truly great men of the Bible. He was Israel's most famous king; in fact, a few years ago, his name and likeness were plastered all over modern Israel during the national celebration of the three thousandth anniversary of his birth. His name appears in Scripture over one thousand times—more frequently than that of any other biblical character. He was a faithful shepherd, a skilled musician, a gifted composer, a courageous warrior, an able administrator, and a king of renown.

Yet David was a man just like us: a man who struggled, who faced challenging giants; Goliath was just one of many. People often overlook the fact that the biggest giants David faced were rejection, anger, depression, and moral failure—giants much more difficult to defeat than Goliath. With God on his side, however, David was ultimately able to defeat every giant life put before him.

As we consider his experience, we'll be able to identify a number of important lessons from the past, lessons that will help us take on the giants in our lives today.

Beyond the Physical Giants

The authors of this book have spoken with countless people over the years who struggle with intense feelings of rejection. Some of them would really surprise you: they are sharp, talented, and spiritually astute. You would assume they possess a great deal of self-confidence and trust in the Lord. Yet they struggle with rejection big-time.

Scripture doesn't tell us whether David struggled with feelings of rejection. We simply observe in the Bible that he was rejected. In fact, David experienced three kinds of rejection: his father's passive rejection, his brother's active rejection, and his boss's ongoing rejection.

First, let's consider David's passive rejection at the hands of his father, Jesse. We find evidence for this rejection in 1 Samuel 16. The Lord had just told Samuel that he had rejected Saul as king over Israel. Then God instructed Samuel to call Jesse's clan together in Bethlehem and anoint a king from among his sons. A special sacrificial meal was held—an event unlike any in our culture but one that was a big deal in Israel. Because Samuel was the judge of all the people, the equivalent of the president or the prime minister today, the event would have been similar to such an official inviting you and your family to a special get-together. Jesse was present, along with Samuel and Eliab, Jesse's oldest son; in fact, seven of Jesse's sons were present.

When he saw Jesse's firstborn, Samuel immediately concluded that he was the man. As his hand was about to lift the flask of oil to anoint Eliab, the Lord told the prophet, "Do not look at his appearance or at his physical stature, because I have refused him. For the LORD does not see as man sees; for man looks at the outward appearance, but the LORD looks at the heart" (16:7). Modern medicine has developed some amazing tools for diagnosis, including X rays, CAT scans, and magnetic resonance imaging. They can literally look into a person's body using a noninvasive procedure and tell what's going on inside, even to the point of detecting the presence and size of a tumor. Similarly, God was able to look beneath the surface of Eliab and pinpoint strategic weaknesses in this young man's heart. David, on the other hand, had already been recognized as "a man after [God's] own heart" (1 Samuel 13:14; compare Acts 13:22), a man whose passion in life was to love and walk with the Lord God.

But back to this matter of rejection. When we examine the record of guests who signed the register at this festive occasion in 1 Samuel 16, David's name is nowhere to be found. Samuel even asked Jesse, "Are all the young men here?" (v. 11). Someone was missing. While the rest of the family partied with the prophet, David, the youngest, found himself stuck with the sheep.

We all understand how this works. The youngest in the family is often assigned the most menial chores. Many people, as the youngest, felt rejected. But David's family, it seems, acted like he existed only to care for the animals. One of two things happened: either Jesse forgot David, or worse, the father intentionally left his youngest son out.

Perhaps you can connect with what happened to David. Maybe there was a time when your family held a special event and someone forgot to include you or chose to leave you out altogether. It hurts, doesn't it? Even for mature Christian adults, being left out at church, at work, or even in our families can be very painful.

Sibling Rejection, Verbal Insult

Jesse wasn't the only one to reject David; the young shepherd also clashed horribly with his own brother, Eliab, just before he took on Goliath. Eliab and two of his siblings had enlisted in Saul's army; and Jesse asked David to check on his brothers and to take them dry grain, loaves of bread, and cheeses. It was a simple, straightforward assignment, and David handled it well. He had just arrived at the battle site in the Valley of Elah and boldly asked, "Who is this uncircumcised Philistine that he should defy the armies of the living God?" (17:26).

Upon hearing this, Eliab's anger burned against his younger brother. He replied with bitter insult: "Why did you come down here? And with whom have you left those few sheep in the wilderness? I know your pride and the insolence of your heart, for you have come down to see the battle" (17:28).

Makes you think of the old schoolyard rhyme: Sticks and stones may break my bones but words will never harm me. Whoever wrote that was totally wrong. You don't have to hit somebody to batter him. Eliab's words were shattering, and perhaps you can still hear the echo of someone you love letting you know, in no uncertain terms, how incompetent, irrelevant, and immaterial you are as a person. Eliab didn't leave many stones unturned in his attempt to insult his younger brother.

Some time ago a friend named Paula phoned to check on her father, who was seriously ill. Her mother answered the phone, and Paula can remember to this day hearing her father ask, "Marge, who is it?" Paula's mother replied, "It's your daughter." You can imagine the incredible pain Paula felt when she heard her father's response, "Tell whoever's calling I only have one daughter, and she's here in the room with me." As Paula later explained, even though she understood her dad's reaction intellectually, because he had always seemed to favor her sister and the two of them experienced numerous personality clashes over the years, it nonetheless took her months to get over the emotional blow of that bitter conversation.

Perhaps Paula would take heart in knowing that even though David's father and brother rejected him harshly, the Lord God chose him. That's what Psalm 78:70, 71 points out:

> He also chose David His servant,
> And took him from the sheepfolds;
> From following the ewes that had young He brought him,
> To shepherd Jacob his people,
> > And Israel his inheritance.

Nevertheless, rejection by those close to us, whether passive like Jesse's or active like Eliab's, hurts. But David had yet another rejection to experience: the ongoing jealousy and hatred of the man to whom he reported, his boss, who in his culture was his king. And Saul's rejection of David ultimately led to outright opposition.

Goliath and Saul: Hostility and Jealousy

Before he felt the heat of Saul's opposition, however, David faced the threat of a giant who would have towered over today's professional basketball superstars. Almost ten feet tall, Goliath carried a spear, with an iron head weighing seventeen pounds. No young man ever faced a more formidable foe.

Yet we all know how the story turned out. Disdaining Saul's armor, David selected five smooth stones—there's no explanation why he picked five, although Goliath was reported to have had four brothers. After the Philistine taunted the young man, saying, "I will give your flesh to the birds of the air and the beasts of the field," David replied courageously, "You come to me with a sword, with a spear, and with a javelin. But I come to you in the name of the LORD of hosts, the God of the armies of Israel, whom you have defied. This day the LORD will deliver you into my hand . . . that all the earth may know that there is a God in Israel . . . the battle is the LORD's" (17:45–47).

Instead of running away, as he might have been tempted to do, David hurried toward the Philistine army to meet his opponent. He put his hand into his bag, took out a stone, and hurled it, striking the Philistine on his forehead. Then he dispatched Goliath with the giant's own sword. It was an incredible victory, against impossible odds. And the same God who helped David promises victory to us today.

The opposition David faced from Goliath constituted an immediate threat. The opposition he encountered at the hand of Saul, though just as dangerous, was spread out over several years. Following his victory over Goliath, Saul invited David to join his warriors. In doing so, "[David] behaved wisely. And Saul set him over the men of war, and he was accepted in the sight of all the people, and also in the sight of Saul's servants" (18:5). With his popularity growing, his life had momentum; David was headed upward on a fast track.

That is exactly when opposition reared its ugly head, as so often happens. Its root was jealousy. When King Saul—an imposing physical specimen who stood head and shoulders above the people (9:2)—heard the Israelite women sing, "Saul has slain his thousands, and David his ten thousands," he went ballistic (18:17). "What more can he get but the kingdom?" he mused. And from that day onward, Saul kept a jealous eye on David (18:8, 9 NIV).

Coupled with his suspicion, Saul felt an intense fear, a fear that David would indeed displace him. Perhaps he recalled the words of Samuel, who had predicted that God intended to remove Saul and replace him with a man after God's own heart.

It doesn't take a lot of experience or brilliance to figure out how jealousy can lead to opposition. If we are honest about it, we all have to admit to some occasional struggles with the emotion Shakespeare described as a "green-eyed monster."[1]

Saul's jealous hostility expressed itself in a variety of ways. First, he attempted to pin David to the wall with his spear. When that failed, he offered his daughter in marriage to David in exchange for evidence that David had slain a hundred Philistines. When the young man successfully dispatched two hundred of Israel's enemies, Saul grew still more afraid of David and "became David's enemy continually" (18:29). Yet David continued, despite this opposition, to "behave wisely in all his ways, and the LORD was with him" (18:14).

Hostile opposition can come from someone we know, even someone we respect—as happened to David with Saul. It can also occur despite our doing the right thing.

John, a corporate vice president, made the decision to purchase some equipment for the company where he worked, equipment needed for the production process. But some within the organization weren't happy with John. After all, they had worked for the organization longer than he, and they were irritated by steps he had taken to streamline the company's operation. Though they claimed to be his friends, they criticized his actions to the executive vice president and chief operating officer, and they were almost successful in having him fired for authorizing the equipment purchase. John's job was spared only because he had had the forethought to secure the approval of the CEO and the company's legal counsel before deciding to make the purchase.

Not only can opposition come from those we know and respect, it can happen despite our doing the right thing; opposition can strike suddenly and unexpectedly, almost like a tornado. One day when David stood before Saul to play the lyre, he wound up dodging the king's spear (19:10). He probably didn't have a clue when he awakened that morning that this would be the day when the man under whom he served would nearly take his life. We may not be prepared for the opposition that arises suddenly and places us in harm's way, but we need to be alert to its possibility without failing to trust the Lord for grace and wisdom when it comes.

More Giants to Slay

Rejection and opposition were not the only giants David faced then and we encounter today. He dealt with several others, including anger, depression, and failure. David's most notable experience with the giant of anger occurred during a time of turmoil in Israel. 1 Samuel 25 records that after Samuel died, a wealthy landowner named Nabal of Maon insulted David after he and his followers had provided protection for Nabal's flocks. Perhaps you've had a similar experience. You expected someone to greet you warmly and to express appreciation for help you provided. Instead, they acted like you didn't even exist, or worse, as though you were their enemy.

When Nabal insulted David, the son of Jesse became furious. When his men reported the insult, he announced, "Every man gird on his sword" (25:13). In our day we might have heard David saying, "Go ahead, Nabal, make my day."

His anger at a boiling point, David took four hundred of his men, fully intending to wipe out Nabal and all who were with him. Had Nabal's wife, Abigail, not intervened and deftly deflected David's anger, he might have committed an act that would have kept him from becoming Israel's king. It's ironic that the same man who expressed such restraint toward Saul, refusing to "stretch out [his] hand against . . . the LORD's anointed" (24:10), could set out so quickly to get revenge against Nabal.

Without question, anger is a giant that can jump us unexpectedly from any direction. It can motivate peaceful individuals, even the godly, to say and do things that are totally out of harmony with Christian character. Perhaps anger is one of the giants with which you've struggled. If so, there is hope. God's Spirit can enable us to obey the prompting of Ephesians 4:26, 27, which reminds us, "Be angry, and do not sin; do not let the sun go down on your wrath, nor give place to the devil." After all, the fruit of the Spirit includes self-control (Galatians 5:22, 23).

David and Depression

David also struggled from time to time with the giant of depression. A man of extreme highs, he could feel so low at times it was as though he had to reach up to touch bottom.

Most of us probably don't think of David as ever being depressed. After all, he was so positive and upbeat about taking on Goliath and he was able to weather Saul's scathing attacks. He consolidated the kingdom, then graciously extended support and friendship to the son of his friend Jonathan, Mephibosheth (2 Samuel 9:1–13). This act of kindness is remarkable because the young man, who was lame and unable to care for himself, could have been considered a rival—he was, after all, Saul's grandson—and either banished or even put to death under the custom of that day.

Truly, David's successes were many. Yet when we read Psalms 22, 42, or 43, we discover David feeling abandoned, ("My God, why have You forsaken Me?"), loathing himself ("I am a worm, and no man, a reproach of men"), and viewing himself as though under attack by angry bulls, a roaring lion, and vicious dogs (Psalm 22: 12–17).

Following his adultery with Bathsheba (which we'll explore in more detail later), David was overwhelmed by depression and guilt. Psalm 32 provides clear insight into his sense of despair, which the freedom of God's forgiveness enabled him to overcome. Perhaps you have struggled with depression, felt its giant footprints weighing you down. Its cause may have been abuse in childhood, guilt over sinful actions on your part, physical causes, or a combination of factors. Whatever the case, as David discovered, there is hope, even for the seriously depressed. "Why are you cast down, O my soul? And why are you disquieted within me?" he wrote. "Hope in God; for I shall yet praise Him, the help of my countenance and my God" (Psalms 42:11; 43:5).

Moral Failure

The final giant in David's experience is the giant of moral failure. When confronted with sexual temptation, the man who so often had defeated life's giants failed miserably.

The story, like the account of David's victory over Goliath, is a familiar one. At the peak of his career, with a string of triumphs behind him, David decided to remain behind at his palace one spring when Joab led the Israelite army into battle against the Ammonites. He spied on Bathsheba, the wife of Uriah the Hittite (who was one of David's elite corps of bodyguards), as she bathed. He began an affair with her, then carried out a major cover-up that led to the death of his friend Uriah (2 Samuel 11:1–27).

After months of David's struggles with guilt-induced depression, God sent Nathan the prophet, a longtime friend, to confront the king. When David responded by confessing, "I have sinned against the LORD" (2 Samuel 12:13), God announced through Nathan that the king's life would be spared. Yet the consequences of David's failure would be severe, to himself, his family, and the nation.

Unfortunately, many of God's choice servants today have succumbed to the giant of failure, moral or otherwise, and reaped a whirlwind of devastation. Without question moral failure is a giant against which we must maintain constant vigilance. As Paul warned in 1 Corinthians 10:12, "Let him who thinks he stands, take heed lest he fall."

Resources for Defeating Giants

So many times a major failure, moral or otherwise, can leave us branded a total failure, either in our own eyes or in the sight of others. Yet even considering this major disaster in his life, David still stood triumphant overall against life's giants. Though he struggled fiercely with them, and most were not as easy to overcome as Goliath, nonetheless we consider David an example of vigilance and victory that we should follow.

So what are the resources David used to defeat life's giants? Let's consider ten briefly, with a view to seeing how we can employ them in our lives today.

First, David throughout his life demonstrated integrity and a heart for God. His passion for the Lord is expressed in the words of Psalm 42:1, 2: "As the deer pants for the water brooks, so pants my soul for You, O God. My soul thirsts for God, for the living God. When shall I come and appear before God?" Anyone who has ever felt intensely thirsty for water should be able to grasp what David was talking about. He cared for nothing more than God's presence and to fellowship with him. When Paul was preaching in the synagogue in Antioch of Pisidia, he placed the divine stamp of approval on David with the words, "He raised up for them David as king, to whom also he gave testimony and said, I have found David the son of Jesse a man after my own heart who will do all my will" (Acts 13:22). Simply put, David stayed close to the Lord and obeyed him. Psalm 78:72 provides this summary of David's career: "So he shepherded them according to the integrity of his heart, and guided them by the skillfulness of his hands." When it comes to facing life's giants, nothing is more basic than cultivating a passion for a close relation with God and the integrity that such a relationship naturally produces. The key to creating such a passion today is to spend significant time with the Lord daily in his Word.

Second, David had developed an appropriate sense of self-worth. These days we hear a lot about cultivating our self-esteem and self-image. It's an area in which we need great balance and a biblical perspective. We can see something of that need for balance in the three key players in the drama of David and Goliath. The Philistine giant demonstrated the kind of arrogant self-esteem that many advocate today; he thought himself indestructible. Saul, on the other hand, showed the kind of paranoid jealousy that can develop in a person who believes himself to have no abilities and views everyone else as a threat. David, however, recognized that God had delivered him in the past when he faced a lion or a bear and that the same God who had cared for him then would save him from the Philistine (1 Samuel 17:37). As Paul explained in Romans 12:3, "For I say, through the grace given me, to everyone who is among you, not to think of himself more highly than he ought to think, but to think soberly [the word carries the idea of a realistic appraisal] as God has dealt to each one a measure of faith."

Third, David demonstrated responsibility in caring for little things. A successful businessman once said, "He who doesn't honor the penny isn't worth a dollar." His point was obvious: the little things really matter. When David's father sent him to check on his three brothers, David, awakened early in the morning, saw to it that his sheep were tended before he discharged the responsibilities his father had given him by bringing provisions to his brothers (1 Samuel 17:20–22). When we care for little things in our lives—like caring for our bodies, paying our bills on time, and keeping our word—we are much less likely to be run over by the giants.

Fourth, David demonstrated enthusiasm and a positive mental outlook. When he reached the Israelites' camp, he first handed the supplies he had brought to the supply keeper, then ran to the army and greeted his brothers (v. 22). Then when a cloud of gloom and fear seemed to cover the camp following the challenge that Goliath issued, David said, "What shall be done for the man who kills this Philistine and takes away the reproach from Israel?" (v. 26). Even after his brother had voiced stern criticism, David said to the king, "Let no man's heart fail because of him [Goliath]; your servant will go and fight with this Philistine" (v. 32). The word *can't* simply had no place in this young man's vocabulary. We would say of him today that he viewed every glass as half full rather than half empty. Of course, David's was not a pie-in-the-sky optimism that was out of touch with reality. Rather, his viewpoint paralleled that of Paul, who wrote, "I can do all things through Christ who strengthens me" (Philippians 4:13). When we face adversity, a positive attitude of trust in Christ can help pull us through.

Fifth, David had demonstrated an ability to avoid distraction and to focus. When Eliab sought to deflect David's interest in taking on the giant by ridiculing and belittling his brother, David's response was "What have I done now? Is there not a cause?" (v. 29). Throughout his discussion with Saul, who considered David unfit to go against the Philistine because he was a youth, the young man maintained his focus on the ultimate goal: ridding the land of the source of such blasphemy against the God of Israel. In a day in which we face multiple distractions, learning to focus can be crucial.

Sixth, David overcame this and other giants because of a willingness to trust God for victory. In his interchange with King Saul and his dialogue with Goliath, David expressed a supreme confidence in the Lord's ability to lead him to triumph. Years later, looking back on his life, the aging king wrote, "I have been young, and now am old; yet I have not seen the righteous forsaken, nor his descendants begging bread" (Psalm 37:25). Throughout his life David's trust in the Lord brought him victory after victory over giants of all kinds. Let's remember: God leads in triumph, and apart from him we can do nothing.

Closely linked with this was David's sense of mission, a seventh resource for defeating life's giants. David saw himself as a representative of the God of Israel. "I come to you in the name of the LORD of hosts, the God of the armies of Israel, whom you have defied," he announced to Goliath. "The LORD will deliver you into my hand, and I will strike you and take your head from you . . . that all the earth may know that there is a God in Israel. Then all this assembly shall know that the LORD does not save with the sword and spear for the battle is the LORD's, and He will give you into our hands"

(1 Samuel 17:45–47). No question, David considered himself a man on a mission. It was a trait he demonstrated throughout his life, and we who are ambassadors for Christ need to cultivate that trait today.

Eighth, David demonstrated a sense of perspective; he didn't puff up with pride after felling Goliath. When Saul demanded to know who he was, he simply answered, "I am the son of your servant Jesse the Bethlehemite" (v. 58). Saul had begun with the same sense of humble perspective. Tragically, he allowed his kingship to go to his head, and he became arrogant and self-willed. One of the dangers we face when we're successful is the temptation to believe that we're responsible for our successes, when the Lord made them possible.

Ninth, and of great significance during the time he was hunted by Saul, David experienced the encouragement of a true friend. Immediately following his encounter with Goliath, we read that "the soul of Jonathan was knit to the soul of David, and Jonathan loved him as his own soul" (1 Samuel 18:1). The two men were the best of friends, forging a covenant between them. Time after time, when David felt the withering heat of discouragement from Saul's relentless attacks, Jonathan provided David a refreshing dose of encouragement. During the days when "Saul sought [David] every day," Jonathan "arose and went to David in the woods and strengthened his hand in God. And he said to him, 'Do not fear, for the hand of Saul my father shall not find you. You shall be king over Israel, and I shall be next to you. Even my father Saul knows that'" (23:14, 16, 17). Each of us desperately needs the encouragement of godly friends if we are to overcome the giants of life. We also need to be giving encouragement. No one modeled the role of encourager more effectively than Jonathan.

David's final resource for defeating life's giants was the patience to wait for God, and he may have expressed this best in the words of Psalm 37:7–9: "Rest in the LORD, and wait patiently for Him; do not fret because of him who prospers in his way, because of the man who brings wicked schemes to pass. Cease from anger, and forsake wrath; do not fret—it only causes harm. For evil doers shall be cut off; but those who wait on the LORD, they shall inherit the earth."

At times we feel the giants are getting the best of us. Yet like David, we can count on the Lord for ultimate victory.

We live in a time when giants continue to roam the earth; and although we may not encounter giants like Goliath, Saul, or even Eliab, we all, at some time or another, face rejection, opposition, anger, depression, or failure. However, if we carefully study and apply the resources David used and his relationship with God, we too can defeat the giants we face in the twenty-first century.

🍃 David 🍃

Take-Away Messages from the Past

1. People tend to judge on outward, initial impressions. God does not.

2. Many times even God's people will follow the majority opinion (the majority in Israel fled from Goliath). God does not always go with the majority but with the one who walks with him and those he chooses. God plus you always constitutes a majority.

3. Some tasks appear impossible. David was outstanding with a slingshot, but it was God who made it work.

4. Past victories (such as David's over the bear and lion while tending sheep) can serve as a springboard for defeating life's giants today.

5. A personal victory over a giant trial in life is wonderful, but there's no room for personal pride or self-congratulations. After all, "The battle is the LORD's" (1 Samuel 17:47).

Choices for Today

1. Name a time in your life when someone judged you too quickly after an initial impression. Ask God to encourage you with his words, "For the LORD does not see as man sees; for man looks at the outward appearance but the LORD looks at the heart" (1 Samuel 16:7).

2. Memorize the following verse to encourage you, "Then Samuel took the horn of oil and anointed him in the midst of his brothers; and the Spirit of the LORD came upon David" (16:13).

3. Memorize and encourage yourself with this verse: "Then David said to the Philistine, 'You come to me with a sword, with a spear, and with a javelin. But I come to you in the name of the LORD of hosts'" (17:45).

4. Remember past victories and encourage yourself with the following verse from 1 Samuel 17:36 as you face different kinds of giants today—an emotional giant: "Your servant has killed both lion and bear; and this uncircumcised Philistine will be like one of them."

5. Memorize and encourage yourself with this verse from 1 Samuel 17:47: "The battle is the LORD's."

Chapter Seven

Solomon

A Wise Man with an Achilles' Heel

Who was the wisest man (other than Christ) who ever lived? Who started his walk with the Lord with great zeal, only to lose his sense of mission later? Who spoke with gifted common sense regarding sexual dangers but went on to have seven hundred wives and three hundred concubines, which ultimately led to his demise? Who gave astute proverbs to his son but did not see his son do well? Who possessed wealth, women, and wine but experienced times of despair that led him to say "vanity of vanities; all is vanity" (Ecclesiastes 1:2)? Who said "he who sins against me wrongs his own soul" (Proverbs 8:36) but went on to personal sin and injury? Who offered wisdom designed "to deliver you from the immoral woman" (Proverbs 5:3) but went on to have many foreign women who turned his heart from the Lord as he built temples to honor their gods? Who was the wisest man who ever lived but suffered with a devastating Achilles' heel? The answer, of course, is Solomon.

Solomon was King David's son. When David grew old in years, God designated Solomon to follow his father to the throne. But this new king realized his inability to govern the people of Israel. Early in his reign, as he offered a sacrifice at the great high place in Gibeon and waited all night there, the Lord appeared to him in a dream. God gave Solomon the opportunity to ask for whatever he wished. Humbly, the young man asked for an "understanding heart" to judge the people so that he might "discern between good and evil." This request pleased his God, and the Lord gave him not only a wise heart, but all the material blessings as well (1 Kings 3:4–13).

The wisdom God granted Solomon seems to have pertained to jurisprudence, as we see in his handling of the case of the disputed baby (3:16–27). He identified the real mother in the dispute by threatening to have the child cut in half, then waiting to see which woman would be willing to give the child up to the other to spare its life. We also know that Solomon possessed vast knowledge in the area of natural science (4:33) and a marked intelligence in general (10:1–9).

In the book of Proverbs, we find the demonstration of Solomon's wisdom that perhaps means the most to us, a treasure trove of wisdom for living. Many of the sayings in Proverbs are presented in the form of contrast. Perhaps the overriding contrast is wisdom versus sin:

> Now therefore, listen to me, children,
> For blessed are those who keep my ways.
> Hear instruction and be wise,
> And do not disdain it.
> Blessed is the man who listens to me,
> Watching daily at my gates,
> Waiting at the posts of my doors.
> For whoever finds me finds life,
> And obtains favor from the LORD;
> But he who sins against me wrongs his own soul;
> All those who hate me love death (8:32–36).

These sayings provide practical guidelines for successful living, covering many facets of human life such as marriage, adultery, and parent-child relationships, as well as topics like anger, alcohol, and anxiety. Let's look at some of these more closely, noting the differences in how secular and Christian counseling would approach each.

Marriage

He who finds a wife finds a good *thing*,
And obtains favor from the LORD.

—Proverbs 18:22

A secular marriage counselor doing premarital counseling would most likely encourage both members of a young couple to look at the future mate realistically—to see the person's faults as well as good points. The counselor also probably would stress the importance of accepting that future partner the way he or she is. Although this is good, it lacks some important elements. Proverbs, on the other hand, encourages actively seeking out the right kind of mate to begin with. Proverbs says that a man who "finds a wife finds a good thing" (18:22a). First, note that the word *thing* is not in the Hebrew; a wife is not a thing. The Hebrew says, "He who finds a wife finds good." The word *good* (Hebrew *towb*) carries the idea of being cheerful, kindly, or gracious. Too often men (and in our society today, women as well) primarily consider outward appearances. Yet Proverbs 31:30 warns, "Charm is deceitful and beauty is passing, but a woman who fears the LORD, she shall be praised."

If you start with the right kind of marriage material to begin with, it's much easier to construct a relationship that will last. Yes, it's wise to accept a person as he or she is, but if you seek someone who fits the description of Proverbs 18:22, accepting him or her is not all that difficult to do.

Solomon also warns repeatedly about the frustration of a marriage to a "contentious" person (21:19; 26:21; 27:15). A secular counselor might point out potential problems, but Solomon goes even further, saying, in essence, "Don't do it." In our counseling we always find it surprising to discover couples who admit to a stormy premarital relationship but want to get married anyway. If contentiousness is present before marriage, saying "I do" isn't going to help. It's not unusual to find those same couples seeking marital counseling or even a divorce a few years down the line. Solomon recommends dropping a contentious man or woman like a hot potato!

Adultery

Let your fountain be blessed,
And rejoice with the wife of your youth.
As a loving deer and a graceful doe,
Let her breasts satisfy you at all times;
And always be enraptured with her love.
For why should you, my son, be enraptured by an
    immoral woman,
And be embraced in the arms of a seductress?
For the ways of a man are before the eyes of the
    LORD,
And He ponders all his paths.
His own iniquities entrap the wicked man,
And he is caught in the cords of his sin.
He shall die for lack of instruction,
And in the greatness of his folly he shall go astray.
—*Proverbs 5:18–23*

Secular counseling and Proverbs take divergent paths in many aspects of this issue, perhaps more than on most other topics. Psychology has moved toward what some might call a relative standard. Many secular counselors are more likely to say that intercourse between consenting people is fine as long as they love each other and are not hurting each other. Of course, Scripture takes an absolute position and forbids sex outside marriage without exception.

Most secular counselors focus on the emotional damage adultery and other secrets can cause in a marriage, rather than the immorality of the act itself. They fail to take into consideration the fact that someone knows all our secrets, whether our spouse does or not. It may have come as a surprise to many when Katherine Hepburn, who died on June 29, 2003, at the age of ninety-six, revealed that she had carried on a twenty-seven-year adulterous relationship with Spencer Tracy.[1] But God knew. Solomon said, "For the ways of man are before the eyes of the LORD, and He ponders all his paths" (Proverbs 5:21).

Adultery has consequences far beyond what a secular counselor might consider. Solomon says, "He shall die for lack of instruction" (5:23). There is, of course, the possibility of physical death. According to the American Social Health Association, fifteen million adults are infected with sexually transmitted diseases each year.[2] Not only do these diseases bring shame and physical discomfort, many of them (such as AIDS) can have fatal consequences.

The sin of adultery also causes spiritual damage. The prophet Isaiah confronts the nation of Israel with its sins and says, "But your iniquities have separated you from your God; and your sins have hidden His face from you, so that He will not hear" (Isaiah 59:2). The same is true of God's people today. We can't walk in fellowship with the Lord and walk in sin at the same time.

Anxiety

> Anxiety in the heart of man causes depression,
> But a good word makes it glad.
>
> —*Proverbs 12:25*

Psychology and Proverbs agree on some aspects of anxiety. Both note that anxiety wears on people, often leading to depression. Both conclude that a lack of anxiety and the presence of joy promote health. However, the book of Proverbs tells us a remarkable way to avoid anxiety, addressing the subject far more deeply than does any proposal for psychological treatment. Solomon says, "But a good word makes [the heart] glad" (12:25b).

Proverbs indicates that an anxious heart needs to hear a "good word." There is no better word, however, than God's Word. Depression stemming from anxiety can be effectively dealt with by a steady dose of God's Word seasoned with believing prayer. The Apostle

Paul says in Philippians 4:6–7: "Be anxious for nothing, but in everything by prayer and supplication, with thanksgiving, let your requests be made known to God; and the peace of God, which surpasses all understanding, will guard your hearts and minds through Christ Jesus." Christians have an option that the secular world can't even begin to understand. They have the Good Book, which contains all the good words they need to deal with anxiety—plus the resource of prayer!

Anger

A patient man has great understanding,
But a quick-tempered man displays folly.
—*Proverbs 14:29 (NIV)*

Secular counselors work with many people who are extremely passive and turn most of their anger inward, dealing with it in what are commonly identified as passive-aggressive ways. Yet being passive-aggressive is wrong, just as being overtly aggressive is wrong. However, it seems that in the attempt to help individuals deal with their anger in a healthier manner, the pendulum often swings too far. "Just get it out," secular counselors often advise. In Proverbs we note a repeated emphasis on controlling anger.

Turning anger inward admittedly can lead to physical problems such as ulcers as well as emotional problems like depression. Studies have shown, however, that expressing anger actually can lead to even more anger. The alternative is to give our anger to the Lord. Romans 8:28 says, "And we know that all things work together for good to those who love God, to those who are the called according to His purpose." All the injustices of life that make us so angry can be put in proper perspective when we trust God to use them to accomplish his purpose in our lives. As Christians, we neither have to turn our anger inwardly nor vent it on the people around us; instead, we can channel it through God's purposes to achieve a positive outcome.

Parent-Child Issues

He who spares his rod hates his son,
But he who loves him disciplines him promptly.
—Proverbs 13:24

A few years ago psychology moved away from an emphasis on discipline and more toward one of reason and understanding . . . even leniency. The secular pendulum has recently swung back to the importance of discipline in raising respectful, happy and drug-free children in today's world. Although reason and understanding are extremely important, we note in Proverbs a repeated emphasis on the importance of discipline. Some professionals today agree: Revetta Bowers heads the Center for Early Education in Los Angeles. She says schools are replacing parents. "Schools now make rules, which in many instances are the only rules that are not open to arbitration or negotiation. What children really need is guidance and love and support. We expect them to act more and more like adults, while we act more and more like children. Then, when we're ready to act like parents, they bristle at the retaking of authority."[3]

Bottom line: Solomon's call for timely discipline of children is still the best approach today (Proverbs 19:18).

Intoxication

Wine is a mocker, strong drink is a brawler,
And whoever is led astray by it is not wise.
—Proverbs 20:1

Psychiatry and psychology also point out the dangers of intoxication with alcohol and drugs. According to one article, "Approximately two-thirds of American adults drink an alcoholic beverage during the course of a year, and at least 13.8 million Americans develop problems associated with drinking." The article goes on to state:

Fifty percent of homicides are alcohol related. Forty percent of assaults are alcohol related. One hundred thousand Americans die of alcohol problems each year. More than 40 percent of those who start drinking at age 14 or younger become alcoholic. In 1998, the cost of alcohol abuse was over 185 billion dollars. Over many years of following alcohol and drug use, studies find that 80 percent of high school seniors have tried alcohol, 32 percent have gotten drunk in the last thirty days, 49 percent have smoked marijuana and 63 percent have smoked cigarettes. The average 18-year-old has seen 100,000 television commercials encouraging him or her to drink. The patients who are most vulnerable to excessive alcohol and drug abuse are young adults between the ages of 18–25. They have the highest incidence of alcohol and drug use, but no age group is omitted from falling victim to the problem. More alcoholism is being found in the elderly now that more baby boomers are retiring. Classical alcoholism takes about 15 years to develop, but it can happen much quicker in adolescents and young adults.[4]

But secular counselors weren't the first to recognize the dangers of intoxication and alcoholism. A good description of medical and psychological symptoms can be found in Proverbs 23:30–35. The contrast is best seen in Proverbs 20:1b: "Whoever is led astray by it is not wise." Psychology views it as a disease; Proverbs views it as a lack of wisdom. Psychology stresses the underlying intrapsychic conflicts; Proverbs stresses the choice involved and urges one not to become intoxicated.

Counselors

The way of a fool is right in his own eyes,
But he who heeds counsel is wise.
—*Proverbs 12:15*

A man has joy by the answer of his mouth,
And a word spoken in due season, how good it is!
(15:23).

Pleasant words are like a honeycomb,
Sweetness to the soul and health to the bones
(16:24).

What is desired in a man is kindness,
And a poor man is better than a liar (19:22).

Plans are established by counsel;
By wise counsel wage war (20:18).

When individuals' lives are affected by issues such as marital infidelity, addiction, or parent-child conflicts, the response of both Christians and the population in general is frequently to seek professional counseling. The book of Proverbs provides an excellent resource for determining what constitutes a good or effective counselor. For example, a good counselor is one who has the discernment to know when to speak and when not to speak; he or she knows the importance of a "timely word" (15:23 NIV).

Further, the many different forms of psychotherapies usually have certain common denominators. One of the most important common denominators is support or "pleasant words," as Proverbs 16:24 says.

In addition, successful counselors are consistently considered to have certain traits (empathy, nonpossessive warmth) or as Proverbs 19:22 simply says: "kindness."

Finally, research has revealed that a group solution to a problem is almost always superior to the solution that a single individual can reach. As Proverbs 15:22 would phrase it: "Without counsel, plans go awry, but in the multitude of counselors they are established."

Solomon's wisdom was profound, but what was his Achilles' heel?

Solomon's Achilles' Heel

Solomon's primary sin was disobeying God's commandments by marrying many foreign women. God warned Israel, "Nor shall you make marriages with them. You shall not give your daughter to their son, nor take their daughter for your son. For they will turn your sons away from following Me, to serve other gods; so the anger of the LORD will be aroused against you and destroy you suddenly" (Deuteronomy 7:3, 4). And again: "You shall make no covenant with them, nor with their gods. They shall not dwell in your land, lest they make you sin against Me. For if you serve their gods, it will surely be a snare to you" (Exodus 23:32, 33).

The result of Solomon's primary sin of marrying many foreign women was the secondary sin of worshiping other gods (1 Kings 11:2; Exodus 23:32, 33). Thus, God's warning not to associate with them because they would turn the Israelites' hearts away from him was right on target.

The same issue is of critical importance to Christians and their families today. In 2 Corinthians 6:14 the Apostle Paul warns, "Do not be unequally yoked together with unbelievers. For what fellowship has righteous with lawlessness? And what communion has light with darkness?" Although Paul may have had other issues regarding alliances of believers and unbelievers in mind, it seems clear that his primary concern has to do with the "yoke" of marriage. The three of us have encountered a significant number of individuals who have struggled in their lives because of marriage to an unbeliever, and all too frequently the result is that the unbeliever turns the Christian's heart away from the Lord, rather than vice versa.

There are numerous reasons for Solomon's decline into personally sinful behavior:

His marriages were politically and materially advantageous. The international custom of the day was for kings to marry the daughter of foreign rulers for political advantage. Solomon's sin seems to lie in depending on his own ability to maintain a secure kingdom through these alliances and of wanting the material benefits that would result. He may have been driven by lust, while seeking the ego boost from having sex with many women. In Ecclesiastes Solomon notes that he tried numerous ways to find fulfillment in life and did not withhold from himself any pleasure.

He also seemed to want his wives to like him, to the point that he allowed them to worship their own gods. He never confronted any of them for their idolatry, and he even indulged in some worship of their gods himself (1 Kings 11:5).

Solomon may have drifted away from the habit of spending regular time in God's Word, making him more vulnerable to temptation. The Word notes that "his heart had turned from the LORD God of Israel" (1 Kings 11:9; compare Psalm 119:11).

If we're not careful, we may find ourselves susceptible to the same pitfalls that tripped up the wise king Solomon. We may be tempted to depend on our own ability to maintain recognition and security rather than trusting God. Or we may find ourselves motivated by lust and draw away from God by the sexual temptations that have become so prevalent in our society. We may even fall into the trap of wanting those around us to like us, to the point where we wind up compromising our spiritual convictions.

Walking the Talk

It's easy to become disillusioned when what people say is different from what they do. Have you ever felt that way toward other Christians? Consider the many contrasts between what Solomon said and what he did. Does it seem similar to what you experience with Christians today? When Christians don't walk the talk, their actions may disillusion others.

Perhaps Brad could relate to that kind of disillusionment. He had just completed his MBA when two Christian friends, Mark and Walter, invited him to join them in a new business venture. Brad was hesitant at first—after all, both Mark and Walter were older, more experienced, and more spiritually mature. Yet after praying about it with his wife, Cindy, and discussing it with his pastor and some friends at church, Brad decided to make the commitment.

When the three men met to sign papers in Walter's attorney's office, Brad thanked them for the opportunity to be involved in a business that was to be operated on Christian principles and for the chance to work with men of integrity.

However, Brad was soon confronted with a sad reality. Within a year he discovered that his partners were cooking the books.

Brad didn't know what to do. So he called a meeting with his partners to confront them. Their response: "Everyone's doing it, Brad. Don't be naive. There isn't a company in our business that doesn't fudge on its books. After all, we'll have more money to give to the Lord's work if we avoid paying those taxes."

When it came time to file the appropriate tax forms, Brad's conscience wouldn't let him sign off on the papers. He alerted the tax authorities, who carried out a thorough audit. As a result, the company wound up facing severe penalties and eventually went bankrupt.

How did Brad's pastor and his Christian friends respond? Were they supportive?

None of them ever called to encourage Brad. In fact, most of them gave him the cold shoulder at church. Those who did speak asked him why he turned against his partners.

Question after question ran through Brad's mind. *Did my colleagues really believe what they had been preaching? Did they sell out their integrity for the chance to make more money? Was financial security more important to them than doing what the Word of God says? How could they preach one thing and do the opposite? Had they been walking in fellowship with Christ at one point but come to rationalize sinful behavior?*

How could someone in Brad's shoes cope with this kind of situation? For one thing Solomon's take-away messages could have provided him with significant help. Brad also could have learned that one must sometimes do as Solomon's father, David, once did and encourage himself in the Lord when others were not there for him (1 Samuel 30:6). After all, following Christ and obeying his word is an individual choice, not a community decision.

🌿 Solomon 🌿

Take-Away Messages from the Past

1. Solomon was given wisdom in response to his asking. The same wisdom is available to us (James 1:5, 6).
2. Solomon had trouble setting boundaries for himself (sexual) and others (allowed his wives to worship other gods).
3. A warning was given to future generations that we should follow God even when those around us do not, even godly leaders like Solomon (Joshua 24:15; 1 Corinthians 16:13, 14; 1 Timothy 4:12–16).
4. Accountability is a vital necessity for leaders like Solomon; when it isn't present, disaster can result (Hebrews 3:13).
5. Solomon seemed oblivious to the temptations he was surrounded with, and ultimately he succumbed (1 Corinthians 10:12).

Choices for Today

1. Have you specifically asked God for wisdom? James 1:5, 6 invites us to do so, but warns us to ask in faith.
2. Select one healthy boundary you will draw today for yourself or others.
3. Name one instance when you were disillusioned with other Christians around you. How might you have responded differently?
4. Do you have one or more individuals to whom you are accountable? If not, find someone and establish an accountability relationship.
5. Memorize and meditate on 1 Corinthians 10:12 and 13 to keep yourself aware of the danger and the solution.

Chapter Eight

Elijah

Committed but Not Perfect

Perfectionism is a scourge that many of us have had to deal with since childhood. C. Markham Berry provides a graphic description of this way of thinking in his contribution to an anthology of Christianity and psychotherapy. "Man finds the concept of the ideal, that internalized measure of the utterly perfect, both his best friend and his greatest tormentor. At one moment it seems good and is seen in an aura of ultimate reality, and as such is a goal which tantalizes his pride with grandiose promises of becoming the very best . . . in another moment man feels condemned because he falls so short of its standard, and it becomes the anvil upon which the conscience hammers into him depressing guilt and [a] sense of worthlessness."[1]

So how can I tell if I'm a perfectionist? Agreeing with the following statements may tip you off that you have some significant perfectionistic traits:

- If I do not hope for the highest standards of achievement in my performance, I will be a second-rate or a no-rate person.
- If I do not fulfill my hopes of success, I will be rejected by others, shunned and shamed by those I value.
- When I fall short of my hopes, I know deep inside that I am worthless; I am less of a person.
- I hope always to perform well above average because just doing well is no satisfaction at all.

- I hope I will never need admit any fault or error openly before others because people will think less of me.[2]

Perhaps you've come to the conclusion that you are a bit of a perfectionist—maybe even more than a bit! The problem is, we as humans are not perfect and never will be.

Elijah's Bold Entrance

The story of Elijah is a remarkable one, the account of a man raised up by God during a time of moral and spiritual decline. With a sudden, dramatic entrance onto the scene in Israel, the prophet declared, "As the LORD God of Israel lives, before whom I stand, there shall not be dew nor rain these years, except at my word" (1 Kings 17:1). Talk about in-your-face confrontation. Here's a man whose commitment to the Lord, the desire to be God's man in the face of opposition that reached as high as the throne of Israel, provides us with a stirring example of dedication.

Scripture gives us very little of Elijah's background. The key to understanding the man and his mission can be found in his name. The Hebrew name *Elijah* means "my God is Yahweh." That name is significant because the wicked king Ahab and his pagan wife Jezebel had not only sought to introduce the satanic worship of Baal, they were doing everything in their power to stamp out the worship of Yahweh, the Hebrew name translated "the Lord," the personal name for God, in Israel.[3] Commenting on Elijah, biblical scholar and pastor Hampton Keathley notes, "He had developed a character of sojourner, one who was separated from the lifestyle of his day. He was a man with a light grip on the details of life; a man willing and able to pick up and go if God said go. He was not bogged down, chained by his comfort zones or by a desire for the material details of life."[4] In short, the prophet was committed.

Elijah said there would be no rain in Israel (1 Kings 17). So why did the prophet predict—and accurately, we note—that there would be no rain? Because rain is what the Baal worshipers believed their god provided. If Yahweh, the true God that Elijah worshiped, could keep the rain from falling, then the evidence would be clear.

As we follow the narrative of Elijah, we see him walking in obedience to the Word of the Lord, first hiding by the brook Cherith where he was fed by ravens (17:1–6). Then he traveled to Zarephath near the coastal city of Sidon, where he found provision from the hospitality of a widow, then restored her dead son to life through the power of God (17:8–24).

The Prophet Confronts Ahab

As the third year of Elijah's career began, the drought continued. God instructed the prophet to present himself before Ahab, which led to a dramatic confrontation between the prophet of Yahweh and four hundred fifty prophets of Baal (18:20–22). It's a story many of us remember vividly from childhood Sunday school. Two altars were constructed atop Mount Carmel in northeast Israel. The prophets of Baal called out loudly for their god to send fire but received no response. Yahweh's sole prophet instructed the people to pour water over the sacrifice, crying out to the Lord, then watched as fire from Yahweh fell from heaven to consume the burnt sacrifice, the wood, the stones of the altar, and even to lick up the water in the trenches.

What a man! What intense commitment, what great faith, what amazing courage! Yet Elijah was a man just like us. It wasn't that the prophet had no weaknesses, no fear, no struggles. He didn't stand head and shoulders spiritually above everyone else. He was, as James (5:17 NIV) put it, "just like us." That's what we see in 1 Kings 19, following the great victory on Mount Carmel.

The Prophet's Imperfection

When we read 1 Kings 19, it's almost as if Elijah has experienced a major personality transplant. He had been courageous; now he seems fearful. Earlier he called on the Lord God; now he forgets to pray. Previously he stood courageously in the face of his enemies; now he runs for his life. Earlier he carried out ministry to a widow; now he abandons his servant, walks off into the wilderness, and even asks God to take his life!

So what happened to the prophet? After carefully studying this portion of the Elijah narrative, the authors of this book believe that the prophet suddenly came face to face with the fact that he was an imperfect human just like us. And perhaps because he was a perfectionist, he just couldn't handle it.

After the victory of Mount Carmel, Jezebel, who apparently had not been present, sent a message to Elijah declaring her intention to have him assassinated within twenty-four hours (19:1–2). In the vernacular of our day, she put out a contract on the prophet.

It's remarkable to consider what Elijah didn't do. The great man of God didn't pray; he didn't ask God to save him; he didn't stand courageously with a declaration that the God who sent fire from heaven on Mount Carmel would spare his life from Jezebel or anyone else in the capital city of Jezreel.

Instead, terrified, the prophet fled for his life to the other end of Israel (19:3). Ironically, this is the same man who had previously encouraged the widow of Zarepath not to be afraid (17:13).

Reaching the southernmost town in Israel, Beersheba, Elijah left his servant behind and slipped into the desert. Sitting under a broom tree, a relatively small desert bush, he begged God to take his life.

In this request we can see a strong hint of perfectionism. Notice the prophet's words: "It is enough! Now, LORD, take my life, for I am no better than my fathers!" (19:4). Apparently, Elijah's godly ancestors had tried to rid the land of Baal worship. They had not been successful, but Elijah had fully expected to succeed where they had not. And even though he had experienced unparalleled success, the fact that Jezebel remained as a threat to his life and an advocate for Baal worship demonstrated that he had not been perfect in his efforts to bring the nation back to the true God. Exhausted, discouraged, and burned out, the prophet finally fell asleep.

God's Response to Elijah's Despair

At this point we see the loving, gracious hand of the Lord at work to encourage and strengthen his troubled servant. First, the Lord through an angel provided food and water to meet the prophet's physical needs. After all, he had just covered approximately twenty-five miles from Mount Carmel to Jezreel, more than eighty miles from Jezreel to Beersheba, then a day's journey—perhaps fifteen miles—into the desert that today is referred to as the Negev. Isn't it encouraging that God's angel didn't say, "Wake up and preach, Elijah"? Instead, the angel invited the prophet to eat. After that, he was given the opportunity to sleep again, then provided with yet another meal.

After meeting the prophet's physical needs, the Lord next addressed his emotional needs, and God did so much as a modern counselor would do. Twice as the prophet rested in a cave near Mount Horeb, the Lord asked, "What are you doing here Elijah?" (19:9, 13).

In each instance the prophet's reply was the same: "I've been very zealous for the LORD God of hosts, for the children of Israel have forsaken Your covenant, torn down Your altars, and killed Your prophets with a sword. I alone am left; and they seek to take my life" (19:10, 14). So why did the Lord ask twice? The answer lies in the fact that the prophet's deep-seated emotions—fear, anger, and resentment—needed to be drawn out. As the ultimately skilled counselor, the Lord provided this service to his prophet.

After providing for his physical and emotional needs, the Lord next addressed some important spiritual issues with the prophet, who seemed to have forgotten many of the lessons he learned about God's Word and power. Following a strong wind, an earthquake, and a fire, God spoke to the prophet in a "still small voice" (19:12). What was the point? Although God had made himself known in spectacular, powerful demonstrations in the past, he could speak to the prophet quietly and use him in less dramatic ways as well. God's Word was still available to the prophet, and he didn't have to be presiding over a national revival or even carrying on a public ministry to receive a significant word from the Lord. What an important lesson for those of us who are committed to the Lord, yet struggling with our imperfections today!

Finally, the Lord gave the prophet some responsibilities. He did not tell Elijah to go back and confront Jezebel but to anoint three individuals: Jehu as Ahab's successor over Israel, Hazael to be king over Syria, and Elisha to become Elijah's assistant and ultimate successor as prophet. And the Lord reminded Elijah that he was not the only faithful servant of the true God left in Israel; seven thousand had never bowed to the pagan god Baal (19:15–18).

Lessons from the Prophet

So what can we learn from this story of this great prophet that can help us maintain our commitment while dealing with our own imperfections today?

First, Elijah's story teaches us that God uses those who are willing to be committed to him. The one overriding lesson we learn from Elijah's life and ministry is that, because of his commitment, Elijah was God's man—God's tool—to call the nation back to himself.

Elijah's story teaches that God will care for us and bless our ministry. He is there for us, just as he was there for the prophet, both in the early days of Elijah's ministry and after his flight from Jezebel. The prophet discovered God's care and blessing. He learned firsthand the lesson Paul expressed in Romans 8:31: "If God is for us, who can be against us?"

Another lesson we can learn from this godly man is that no one is above failure and that we may even fail in an area of strength. If we used the terminology of the church today to describe Elijah, we'd probably call him a prayer warrior. After all, as James (5:17) reminded us, he "prayed earnestly that it would not rain . . . and it did not." Yet when push came to shove and Jezebel appointed a squad of hit men, the prophet failed to fall to his knees. Instead, in terror he fled for his life. Frequently our own failures come in areas where we are strong, when we seem to forget previous spiritual victories or lessons we've learned.

The prophet's life further teaches that God is the ultimate answer to depression and despair. God's solution included proper rest, nourishment, and mental as well as spiritual help and insight. After all, we are not simply a body, a mind, or just spirit. As Paul reminded the Thessalonian Christians, "May your whole spirit, soul, and body be preserved blameless" (1 Thessalonians 5:23). Our whole being includes all these elements: the spirit, with which we are connected to God; the soul or self-consciousness, including our mind and emotions; and the body, through which we are linked to the world around us. Each is important and worthy of care.

Finally, we learn that even though Elijah experienced a measure of failure, the Lord never gave up on his prophet. God did not write him off because he had run from Jezebel or take him out of service permanently because of his suicidal prayer in the wilderness. Instead, after addressing his needs and wounds, the Lord reconnected with Elijah through the still small voice, then recommissioned him with several important assignments, and even gave him the support of a young prophet he was to mentor. This man, Elisha, would ultimately carry on the legacy of the prophet of the Lord in Israel.

Was Elijah a man of commitment? Without question. Was he perfect? Of course not. Like the prophet, we too face times of discouragement, even failure and despair. Those times may weaken our commitment, especially if we focus on our imperfections. At such times we need to ask the Lord to forgive our failures and let him strengthen our commitment and encourage us (see 1 John 1:9). We need to take steps to care for ourselves physically through adequate rest, food, and exercise. We need to cultivate emotional health by appropriately ventilating our feelings to God and accepting the support of other believers. We need to recognize the vital importance of maintaining our contact with the Lord by paying attention to God's Word and by conversing with him in prayer. Then as we serve him in ways he directs, we need to remember that we are not the only ones serving the Lord. God still has others, even today, who haven't bowed the knee to Baal.

🌿 Elijah 🌿

Take-Away Messages from the Past

1. Our commitment to God is of much greater importance than who we are, who we're related to, or where we came from.

2. A strong commitment to the Lord will not guarantee that we will never fail him. After all, none of us is perfect.

3. Are we willing to pray like Elijah did and call people back to the Lord? Or are we more concerned with our own agenda than with seeing God glorified and people turned to him?

4. We must stand courageously against those who are opposed to the Lord, resting confidently on the promises of God and the assurance of his presence and provision, no matter how desperate the situation.

5. Are we able to hear God speak to us today through his Word, or do we look for dramatic signs as the only evidence of his hand and voice?

6. God will never give us a larger job than what he will equip and empower us to carry out.

Choices for Today

1. Have you settled the issue of your commitment to the Lord?

2. It is vital to recognize that, even though you may be committed to God, you still aren't perfect.

3. Look for opportunities to stand courageously on behalf of the Lord at work, in your school, or in your community.

4. Take advantage of opportunities to encourage those around you toward revival and to share the gospel with those who don't know Jesus Christ as Savior.

5. Memorize and meditate on Scripture to fortify yourself for times of crisis, so that you will be fortified to stand for God rather than fleeing in the face of danger.

6. Make daily time in God's Word a priority; allow God to speak to you in the still small voice of Scripture.

Chapter Nine

Hezekiah

In Pursuit of God

Years ago, Richard D. Barker penned the words to a hymn, "Longing for Jesus," that reflects the deepest desire of many Christians today:

> *I have a longing in my heart for Jesus,*
> *I have a longing in my heart for Him;*
> *Although I know His presence lingers near me,*
> *I have a longing just to see His face.*
> *I have a longing just to walk with Jesus,*
> *I have a longing just to hold His hand;*
> *To know He's there forever near to guide me,*
> *To know His love will never let me go.*
> *Longing, longing for Jesus,*
> *I have a longing in my heart for Him;*
> *Just to be near Him, to feel His presence,*
> *I have a longing in my heart for Him.*

If you asked one hundred people of all religions and walks of life to name three major objectives in their lives, what do you think would be the most common objective? Perhaps it would relate to the family, a job, or financial security.

If you asked one hundred Christians to identify three major objectives in their lives, on the other hand, the most common objectives would probably be quite different. Perhaps theirs would be to learn more about the Bible, be more faithful in prayer, or lead others to Christ. Whatever the specific answer, it probably would have something to do with pursuing God, cultivating and developing a personal relationship with him. This relationship is at the core of the Christian faith: God wants us to be in pursuit of him. He wants us to get to know him.

A. W. Tozer states it beautifully in his book, *The Pursuit of God*:

> You and I are in little (our sins excepted) what God is in large. Being made in his image we have within us the capacity to know him. In our sins we lack only the power. The moment the Spirit has quickened us to life in regeneration our whole being senses its kinship to God and leaps up in joyous recognition. That is the heavenly birth without which we cannot see the kingdom of God. It is, however, not an end but an inception. For now begins the glorious pursuit, the heart's happy exploration of the infinite riches of the Godhead. That is where we begin, I say, but where we stop no man has yet discovered, for there is in the awful and mysterious depths of the Triune God neither limit nor end.[1]

As you read this chapter, take a moment to think about your own hopes and dreams concerning God. How is your "glorious pursuit" going? Reflect on your "heart's happy exploration." How have you worked to cultivate a personal relationship with God?

In Pursuit of God

We need look no further than the story of King Hezekiah to see how God wants all his children to pursue and know him intimately. Hezekiah's motivating force in life was to know God intimately and to be in pursuit of him: "He trusted in the LORD God of Israel, so that after him was none like him among all the kings of Judah, nor who were before him. For he held fast to the LORD; he did not depart from following Him, but kept His commandments, which the LORD had commanded Moses" (2 Kings 18:5, 6).

Hezekiah was the son of King Ahaz. He began his reign in 728 B.C. at the age of twenty-five and reigned for twenty-nine years (18:2). More important, this young king took the exact opposite direction from his father. Whereas Ahaz had been wicked and apostate, King Hezekiah was known as a sincere and devout (although imperfect) king. As a young man, he had witnessed the gradual disintegration of the northern kingdom and the Assyrian conquest of Samaria. Hezekiah realized that Israel's captivity was a result of disobedience, and he determined that he and the southern kingdom (Judah) would be different: they would pursue God. He reopened the temple and called on the Levites to restore the temple worship.

Hezekiah then began an extensive reformation throughout Judah. Second Kings 18:4–5 tells us: "He removed the high places and broke the sacred pillars, cut down the wooden image and broke in pieces the bronze serpent that Moses had made; for until those days the children of Israel burned incense to it, and called it Nehushtan. He trusted in the LORD God of Israel, so that after him was none like him among all the kings of Judah, nor who were before him."

How Did Hezekiah Pursue God?

Knowing God wholeheartedly is our primary goal as Christians. But how can we accomplish this intimate pursuit? King Hezekiah's example is a valuable one, and we can glean specific and important take-away messages from his life and actions.

Self-Control

For one thing, Hezekiah developed self-control; he did not depart from following the Lord. Second Chronicles 30:8 records: "Now do not be stiff-necked, as your fathers were, but yield yourselves to the LORD; and enter His sanctuary, which He has sanctified forever, and serve the LORD your God, that the fierceness of His wrath may turn away from you."

Self-control may be one of our biggest battles. We can identify with George, the father in the comedy *Father of the Bride* (a remake of a 1950 movie with Spencer Tracy), that deals with a father's anxiety about giving his daughter away in marriage. George (played by Steve Martin) narrates the story, focusing heavily on the preparations for and huge expense of the wedding. Always aware of the large sum of money he's spending, George teeters on the brink of rage throughout the movie—to great comic effect.

Mike Conklin wrote in an article for the *Chicago Tribune*:

Anger seems to be epidemic these days. . . . Dr. Emil Coccaro, a researcher and professor of psychiatry at the University of Chicago Hospitals, has been studying anger for several decades. He says that many hotheads suffer from Intermittent Explosive Disorder (IED). Dr. Coccaro is championing a new drug called Depakote, introduced by Abbott Laboratories in 1995. Interestingly, an effort to find volunteers with volatile tempers for the clinical studies has been unproductive. Apparently, few people see their anger as a problem.

"The other day I got into a friend's car and I noticed the visor on the passenger's side was gone," reported Dr. Coccaro. "I asked what happened, and the driver told me, 'Don't get me started on that. My wife ripped it off.' I told him these things are hard to rip off, and he told me, 'Well, she was really angry.'"[2]

We overeat, overwork, overcommit, and some of us even overdo recreation. Road rage, violence in the workplace, and abuses in our homes are all symptoms of a lack of self-control. Finding the ability to keep life in balance seems to escape a large majority of us. And this lack of self-control results in lives that are stressed out and unhealthy.

Hezekiah shows us that nothing should keep us from pursuing the Lord. Jesus tells us in Matthew 6:33, "But seek first the kingdom of God and His righteousness, and all these things shall be added to you." After all, self-control is a fruit of the Spirit (Galatians 5:22, 23).

Take a few moments to see if there is any area in your life that you need to bring under self-control. Ask yourself: Is there some area of my life that I need to change in order to put Jesus first?

Obedience

Hezekiah's life was also marked by obedience. Second Kings 18:6 records that King Hezekiah kept the Lord's commandments. This implies that the king had studied and knew God's commandments. He came to know the Word; he loved it and obeyed it. Someone once said, "Don't throw God the bone of love unless the meat of obedience is on it." How well do you know your Bible? If you know it, are you following what it says?

Holding Fast

Another important clue to the success of Hezekiah's pursuit of God is described by the words "held fast" (18:6; translated "clave" in KJV). The passage recorded that Hezekiah "held fast to the LORD." It's the same Hebrew word found in Genesis 2:24 (KJV), where a man was to "leave his father and mother and cleave unto his wife." The term implies an intimate friendship and a longing to spend time with someone. It further implies enjoyment of that person's presence. It requires actually investing significant time in the relationship. Holding fast to God indicates that we are intensely in pursuit of him. It means that we desire to spend time with him, to talk with him, to walk with him, to know him as an intimate friend.

Second Chronicles 31:21 reveals: "And in every work that he began in the service of the house of God, in the law and in the commandment, to seek his God, he did it with all his heart. So he prospered." King Hezekiah sought God with all his heart. To be in pursuit of God, we must seek him wholeheartedly, determine that we will take the time to build a relationship with him, and get to know him better than any friend here on earth.

Time with and for the Lord

But how do we develop self control and obedience? How can we hold fast to God? Let's find out what the story of Hezekiah teaches us.

Second Chronicles 29:20 states, "Then King Hezekiah rose early, gathered the rulers of the city, and went up to the house of the LORD." King Hezekiah knew that the pursuit of God takes time. After all, developing any friendship takes time. Only as you spend time together with God can closeness grow. People in our day are always trying to find shortcuts to knowing God, so they go off on various tangents to try to pare down the process. Some look to emotional experiences; others seek the more highly visible spiritual gifts. But the truth is that there is no shortcut to knowing God.

How much time did you spend with the Lord this week? King Hezekiah instructed the Levites, "My sons, do not be negligent now, for the LORD has chosen you to stand before Him, to serve Him, and that you should minister to Him and burn incense" (29:11). The king was underscoring the importance of spending time with the Lord. In our daily quiet time, we ought to talk to God just about himself. How much time have you spent during the last week talking to God just about God, telling him how much you appreciate him, how much you appreciate spending time with him, how glad you are that he is your friend?

Giving Praise

Eric Hauck recalls being with his close friend, Christian singer Rich Mullins, in a worship service just a few days before Rich died in a car accident. As Eric explained later when interviewed in the Mullins biography *R. Mullins: An Arrow Pointing to Heaven,* some friends wanted to gather to praise God. They encouraged everyone who had an instrument to bring it and play. Eric recalls that the music sounded awful. Even those who led the singing sang out of tune.

Someone asked Eric and Rich to lead the group for the rest of the evening. Rich went up to the microphone and said, "I love to be in the church. I love to listen to people sing and play with their hearts. In my profession—contemporary Christian music—we worry about being in tune and sounding good. But this music is the music that is the most pleasing to God, because it is so real, and it comes from the hearts of the children of God."[3]

Praise is an important way to draw close to our God, and one key way we offer praise is through song. Hezekiah knew that: "Moreover King Hezekiah and the leaders commanded the Levites to sing praise to the LORD with the words of David and of Asaph the seer. So they sang praises with gladness, and they bowed their heads and worshiped" (2 Chronicles 29:30).

Time spent singing songs to the Lord about himself will aid us in our pursuit of God. It is especially helpful for us to sing songs to the Lord that express our feelings toward him. King Hezekiah sang songs to the Lord as a part of his offering of praise. Use your hymn-book to find songs that allow you to sing directly to the Lord, or listen to contemporary Christian music on radio or CD. Praise him and sing personally to him. This is a joyous friendship you have with him, and your pursuit shouldn't be somber.

He Is in Pursuit of You

It might be tempting to think that God reveals himself intimately to only a select few. Perhaps we may think that a person must reach some sort of spiritual perfection in order to have this privilege. Perhaps you can hear yourself saying, "Sure, Hezekiah achieved an intimate relationship with God, but that doesn't mean I can."

Keep in mind, however, that no human being is perfect, not even Hezekiah. In 2 Kings 20:13 Hezekiah made a major mistake. He exposed all the wealth of Judah to people from "a far country, from Babylon" (v. 14). Later, in 586 B.C., Babylon would capture Judah and all its wealth just as God warned ("nothing shall be left," v. 17).

There may have been many reasons for Hezekiah's failure. Perhaps the problem was pride, or maybe he simply trusted the wrong people. The important fact to remember is that despite his failure and imperfection, he was still a man in pursuit of God—and we can be too.

Despite all our imperfections, God is already in pursuit of us: "For the eyes of the LORD run to and fro throughout the whole earth, to show Himself strong on behalf of those whose heart is loyal to Him" (2 Chronicles 16:9). God examines the earth to see which people are in diligent pursuit of him. To them he reveals himself. With them he develops and cultivates an intimate relationship. That's the kind of relationship King Hezekiah had with God. He was a man in pursuit of God, and with such pursuit God is greatly pleased even today.

❦ Hezekiah ❦

Take-Away Messages from the Past

1. We can pursue a wonderful, close relationship with God through seeking his presence and obeying his Word.
2. God bestowed tremendous blessing on Hezekiah: "The Lord was with him, he prospered wherever he went" (2 Kings 18:7). He had specific prayers answered, even his request that God would extend his life.
3. One can be in pursuit of God and yet make huge mistakes, as Hezekiah did.

Choices for Today

1. What is one specific choice you would make today that could help you in pursuit of God?
2. Choosing to pursue God does not guarantee wealth and extended life. How would you assess the relative value of those items compared with a close and personal relationship with God?
3. If you have any mistakes on your life's record, have you confessed them to secure God's forgiveness? (1 John 1:9). Will you choose to forgive yourself right now and press on in your pursuit of God?

Chapter Ten

Jeremiah

A Man of Many Contrasts

If you were to ask the average church member today to pick out the Bible characters that he or she knows the most about, few would choose Jeremiah. However, we probably have more insight into Jeremiah's personality than into that of any of the other prophets. His book is filled with autobiographical sections known as Jeremiah's confessions.[1] He wrote the lengthy book that bears his name, as well as the book of Lamentations.[2]

Jeremiah's life was filled with contrasts: he showed maturity but had moments of immaturity; he showed dedication and at times reluctance; he was caring but presented a stern message; he was gentle but very tenacious; he showed affection yet seemed inflexible; he wept but offered hope.

Do you ever feel that, like Jeremiah, your life is a study in contrasts and contradictions? Do you see them as insurmountable obstacles to your relationship with God? Do you feel that your own contrasts give you trouble following the Word of God and maintaining an unshakable faith in him? The life of Jeremiah, a man of many contrasts who ultimately succeeded in the eyes of God when facing seemingly insurmountable obstacles, can give you hope for your own walk with the Lord as we study several significant insights and important lessons revealed in his books.

Each of us is a person of contrasts, and often we see this as a stumbling block in our relationship with the Lord. How can I serve the Lord when I'm up one moment and down the next? How can

God even love me when one day I feel I can trust him for whatever comes along, then twenty-four hours later I'm filled with doubt and insecurity? It's no wonder, then, that Jeremiah's life of contrasts and contradictions has applications for us today.

Jeremiah's Life

Jeremiah grew up in the priestly city of Anathoth. He was the son of a priest, Hilkiah. While still a young man, perhaps around age twenty, he was called to be a prophet. He was told that God had appointed him to this ministry even before he had been formed in his mother's womb (Jeremiah 1:5–10).

Jeremiah prophesied during the final years of Judah. Years before, the nation of Israel had split into the northern kingdom, Israel, and the southern kingdom, Judah. The northern kingdom had fallen many years before. In Jeremiah's time Judah was also on the verge of collapse. Jeremiah prophesied during the reign of the last five kings of Judah.

Jeremiah began his ministry during the reign of Judah's good king, Josiah, with whom he enjoyed a cordial relationship. Josiah had instituted the last great revival of God's people in Judah. The book of the Law had been discovered and read to Josiah, and after the young king heard the Law, he repented and instituted a national revival.

But the second part of Jeremiah's life stands in marked contrast. A series of kings and religious leaders arose who rejected God's truth. When Jeremiah shared God's words with them, he was met with severe opposition and persecution. His people and the leaders of the nation rejected and even imprisoned him. King Jehoiakim destroyed Jeremiah's written predictions (Jeremiah 36:21–23). King Zedekiah permitted the prophet to be imprisoned (32:3). The people rejected Jeremiah, and the residents of his hometown tried to kill him (Jeremiah 11:18–23). Even his relatives rejected him (12:6). The chief governor over the Temple of the Lord had him beaten and put in stocks overnight (20:1–3). In fact, the people, the priests, and the false prophets all wanted to put him to death because they thought he was a traitor (26:11).

Jeremiah gave some extremely important prophecies, including a vivid prediction of the Messiah who will ultimately deliver and provide security for Israel (23:5–6); the seventy-year duration of the Babylon captivity (25:11); and the revelation of the new covenant that will ultimately find fulfillment in a messianic millennial kingdom (31:31–34). But Jeremiah suffered for these and other predictions.

A Case Study in Contrasts

Most of us have contrasts within our personality. At times we may be kind, but on certain occasions we express irritation. Or we usually present a calm temperament but occasionally become tense and worried. Jeremiah's life probably presents more contrasts, and in a greater degree, than most of ours do.

Caring but Stern

The prophet was sensitive and sympathetic by nature; but God commanded him to deliver a stern message of judgment to the people of Judah, who had fallen into sin. God's wrath was about to be executed through the Babylonians. Jeremiah sought in vain to turn the people back to God. With dire warning, yet with hope, he declared: "The LORD sent me to prophesy against this house and against this city with all the words that you have heard. Now therefore amend your ways and your doings, and obey the voice of the LORD your God; then the LORD will relent concerning the doom that He has pronounced against you" (26:12–13).

Sad but Joyful

Jeremiah is generally thought of as being sad. He is commonly called the weeping prophet. Although he shed tears of grief over Israel's sin and judgment, he still experienced extreme joy for himself. For example, Jeremiah 15:16 talks about the joy that Jeremiah found in the Word of God: "Your words were found and I ate them, And

Your word was to me the joy and rejoicing of my heart; For I am called by Your name, O LORD God of hosts." He also offered significant hope in a passage that has become a foundation of encouragement for God's people throughout the centuries. Few passages offer as much encouragement or hope as Lamentations 3:21–23: "This I recall to my mind, therefore I have hope. Through the LORD's mercies [lovingkindnesses] we are not consumed, because His compassions fail not. They are new every morning; Great is your faithfulness." Even though we may perceive Jeremiah as a sad individual, he also experienced joy and offered a great deal of hope and help that we can rely on today.

Mature but Immature

The prophet was an extremely spiritually mature person. His maturity showed as he faithfully proclaimed God's message for over forty years. It must have required extreme maturity to preach an unpopular message for decades—a message that prompted wave after wave of rejection. Jeremiah brought his message of impending destruction to the king, and he did so in a day when the other prophets were predicting victory (Jeremiah 28:1–17).

Jeremiah's maturity can also be seen in his deep relationship with the Lord. In Jeremiah 9:23–24 the prophet states: "Thus says the LORD, 'Let not the wise man glory in his wisdom, Let not the mighty man glory in his might; Nor let the rich man glory in his riches; But let him who glories glory in this, that he understands and knows Me, that I am the LORD, exercising lovingkindness, judgment, and righteousness in the earth; for in these I delight,' says the LORD."

Jeremiah's deep spirituality is perhaps nowhere more evident than in a statement by Jesus' disciples at Caesarea Philippi: "When Jesus came into the region of Caesarea Philippi, He asked His disciples, saying, 'Who do men say that I, the Son of Man, am?' So they said, 'Some say John the Baptist, some, Elijah; and others Jeremiah, or one of the prophets'" (Matthew 16:13–14). To have Jesus mistaken for Jeremiah says a great deal about this prophet's spiritual life.

But although no one doubts Jeremiah's mature spirituality, he did have moments of immaturity. At times he became despondent. It was his lifelong complaint to his mother that she had given birth to him (Jeremiah 15:10; 20:14, 17, 18). Although he ministered for over forty years, the record shows that at times he became reluctant and wanted to quit (Jeremiah 1:6). A list of Jeremiah's afflictions prepared by Bible scholar Charles Dyer also reflects some areas of immaturity: feeling confusion (chapters 2 and 3); feeling miserable (chapter 4); experiencing hardship (chapter 5); having no freedom (chapters 6 and 7); having no prayer or hope (chapter 8); being pursued (chapter 10); feeling torn up (chapter 11); being persecuted (chapter 12); being embarrassed (chapter 14); having no peace or happiness (chapter 17); and feeling weak (chapter 18).[3]

Like many today, Jeremiah seemed at times to be carried away with his own sensitivity. When he focused on God and on delivering his message to others, the prophet maintained a sharp focus on his commitment. When he became preoccupied with himself and his adversity, the focus of his mission was not as sharp.

Dedicated but Reluctant

The stern message Jeremiah was commissioned to preach demanded tenacity. He spoke out against murder, adultery, and other idolatrous practices such as burning incense to Baal. This certainly won him no popularity contests.

Hobart Freeman, in *An Introduction to the Old Testament Prophets*, makes this comment about the quality of Jeremiah's ministry: "Fidelity to the Word of God is not merely preaching carefully selected themes in order to please the hearers, nor following some liturgy; it is the proclamation of the whole counsel of God, the threats as well as the promises, the judgments as well as the blessings, the rebukes as well as the condolences, at whatever the personal cost."[4]

Jeremiah was sometimes so deeply wounded by the reaction of those around him that he wished he had never been born (15:10;

20:14, 17). But in spite of his desire to escape from the pain of rejection, he persevered in the task to which God called him.

Lessons for Us

So how can we connect with a prophet who lived many centuries ago, a man of so many contrasts? Let's consider several ways we can benefit from the life of Jeremiah, and especially from his writings.

We're All in This Together

The prophet reminds us, "The heart is deceitful above all things, and desperately wicked: who can know it?" (17:9 KJV). Because of the deceitfulness of our sinful hearts and motives, we too are often people of contrasts. Like Jeremiah, we experience moments of immaturity. In fact, everyone can identify with this aspect of the prophet's life. Frank Minirth has learned from his studies in psychiatry that no individual is totally mature. Everyone has experienced times of despondency. Every Christian who has ever lived has been reluctant to serve at times. Each of us has some psychological blind spots. Only Jesus Christ demonstrated perfection. The ultimate solution for these areas of contrast in our lives can be found in his person.

In modern psychology there can be a temptation to avoid confrontation or always offer hope and encouragement. We must remind ourselves and others that although God offers grace and mercy, he is also a God of justice who at times disciplines his children. God still hates sin, just as he did in Jeremiah's day. Those who refuse to turn from their sin to faith in Christ today will spend eternity separated from God.

Learning to Lean

Psychiatric research shows that each of us has deep feelings of insecurity and inferiority. Perhaps Jeremiah experienced such feelings. Yet God said to the prophet, "Say not, I am a child: for thou shalt go to all that I shall send thee, and whatsoever I command thee thou shalt speak" (1:7 KJV). This verse reminds us that the ministry God has entrusted to us is one that ultimately depends on the Lord, not on our strengths or abilities.

Look for Meaning and Happiness in the Right Place

Professional counselors affirm from experience that everyone seeks meaning and happiness in life. Yet many people seek to drink life's water from broken cisterns that are unable to hold water. So it was in Jeremiah's day: "For my people have committed two evils: they have forsaken me, the fountain of living waters, and hewn themselves cisterns—broken cisterns that can hold no water" (2:13).

We need to spend time drinking the living water in fellowship with Jesus Christ. Only in him can we—or those to whom we minister—find true lasting meaning and happiness.

Expect Spiritual Conflict

Jeremiah described the intensity of the spiritual conflict he felt when he cried out: "O my soul, my soul! I am pained in my very heart! My heart makes a noise in me; I cannot hold my peace, because you have heard, O my soul, the sound of the trumpet, the alarm of war" (4:19).

Like the prophet of old, believers today are not simply drifting through life. We are involved in a spiritual conflict. Not only can being aware of this conflict sharpen our purpose in life, but it can also prepare us for the difficulties we face.

Success in God's Eyes

Jeremiah shared what might be called a description of true success—not as the world defines it but as God does: " 'Let not the wise man glory in his wisdom, let not the mighty man glory in his might, nor

let the rich man glory in his riches; but let him who glories glory in
this, that he understands and knows Me, that I am the LORD, exercising lovingkindness, judgment, and righteousness in the earth. For
in these I delight,' says the LORD" (9:23–24).

Our contemporary world describes success in terms of money,
influence, power, and prestige. God describes success in terms of a
personal, intimate relationship with him.

Security in God

Jeremiah was faced with great personal insecurity due to the changing conditions of his life. Ultimately, he found his security in God.
He declares "LORD, I know the way of man is not in himself; it is
not in man who walks to direct his own steps" (10:23).

It is natural for us all to feel insecure about the future at times
and inadequate to choose our direction in life. How comforting it
is to know that God is in charge, that he cares enough about us as
individuals to personally direct our steps.

Encouraged yet Not Complacent

Another important lesson Jeremiah learned that has practical significance for us today takes the form of a two-edged sword: words
of encouragement regarding God's provision during adversity coupled with a warning against complacency. God declares, "If you
have run with the footmen, and they have wearied you, then how
can you contend with horses? And if in the land of peace, in which
you trusted, they wearied you, then how will you do in the floodplain of the Jordan?" (12:5).

Life includes times of relative stability as well as periods of intense difficulty. During the former we may grow complacent; however, it is important even in the good times to develop spiritual
maturity and a relationship with God that can enable us to face
those periods of adversity with his strength.

Sharing the Good News

Another lesson we can learn from Jeremiah has to do with those times when we are tempted to keep quiet about our relationship with the Lord. The prophet faced this temptation also, yet he says: "But if I say 'I will not mention him or speak any more in his name,' his word is in my heart like a fire, a fire shut up in my bones. I am weary of holding it in; indeed, I cannot" (20:9 NIV).

Like Jeremiah, we may be tempted to avoid speaking up for the Lord on the job or in the marketplace. Yet when we are walking in fellowship with him and meditating on his Word, we will find it natural to "give an answer to every one" (1 Peter 3:15 NIV).

Trusting God for Good

Jeremiah faced the destruction of his nation and the deaths of many of his countrymen, yet he believed that God ultimately intended good for his people. The Lord says through the prophet, "For I know the thoughts that I think toward you, says the LORD, thoughts of peace and not of evil, to give you a future and a hope. Then you will call upon Me and go and pray to Me, and I will listen to you" (Jeremiah 29:11–12).

Just as God loved Israel with an unceasing love and expressed that love through the prophet, so we can be sure today that he loves us because his intentions are characterized by peace or wholeness rather than evil. We can anticipate that, just as he promised, God will work all things together for good to those who love him (Romans 8:28). Even when he disciplines us, he is proving his ultimate love.

Enduring the Impossible

Sometimes we face circumstances that seem impossible to endure. Two statements from one of the darkest days in Jeremiah's life can provide significant encouragement. "Behold, I am the LORD, the

God of all flesh. Is there anything too hard for Me?" (Jeremiah 32:27). In addition, Jeremiah 33:3 says, "Call to Me, and I will answer you, and show you great and mighty things, which you do not know."

Some humanistic psychiatrists claim that God is only a crutch to lean on. Experience has shown, however, that we all need crutches, and depending on the God who created us is far more reliable than substituting some inferior and ineffective crutch. In his time of greatest adversity, Jeremiah found comfort in God's promise that nothing was too hard for him (32:27) and in God's invitation to call . . . and I shall show you (33:3). God delights in answering prayer, both in the major crises of life as well as in the small, day-to-day challenges we face.

Hopeful in Adversity

Jeremiah's five-chapter book of Lamentations vividly describes the hopelessness of the Jewish captivity. Despite this, the book contains at its midpoint a significant ray of hope. Lamentations 3:21–23 declares: "This I recall to my mind, therefore I have hope. Through the LORD's mercies we are not consumed, because His compassions fail not. They are new every morning; great is Your faithfulness."

God is the same yesterday, today, and forever; so we as his children can rest in the hope that is ours because God is loyal and loving every single day. In this final lesson, Jeremiah again reminds us of the contrast between discouragement or despair and hope that so vividly marked his life.

Stewardship of the Gospel

According to the Apostle Paul, the ultimate test of any person's life is faithfulness. In 1 Corinthians 4:2 he declares: "Moreover it is required in stewards that one be found faithful." Jeremiah was given a calling to communicate God's message. In spite of the contrasts in his life, he was faithful to communicate that message. He loved God's Word, proclaimed it boldly, and endured hardness as a good soldier. Ultimately, it's not the contrasts and contradictions that determine our value; it's our faithfulness to God's calling.

🍃 Jeremiah 🍃

Take-Away Messages from the Past

1. Jeremiah was a man of many contrasts in his life, in his experience, and in his ministry.
2. Jeremiah made the Word of God a significant priority in his life, and he experienced joy as a result.
3. Jeremiah learned that nothing is impossible with God (Jeremiah 32:27).
4. He also learned the vital importance of persistent prayer (33:3).
5. The prophet felt and expressed despair over the destruction of Jerusalem (Lamentations 1 and 2) yet never lost hope in the Lord (3:21–23).

Choices for Today

1. On a scale of zero to ten, with zero being no significant contrast and ten being maximum contrast, how would rate yourself in the contrasts we've observed from the life of Jeremiah? For example, are you caring but stern, sad but joyful, dedicated but sometimes reluctant, usually mature but sometimes immature, affectionate yet at times inflexible?

   Contrasts in life _____
   Contrasts in experience _____
   Contrasts in ministry _____

2. The book of Jeremiah includes a wealth of verses for you to memorize, verses that will stir your heart. Perhaps you might consider memorizing one a month.

   "Can a virgin forget her ornaments, or a bride her attire? Yet My people have forgotten Me days without number" (2:32).

"Therefore thus says the LORD God of hosts: Because you speak this word, behold I will make My words in your mouth fire, and this people wood, and it shall devour them" (5:14).

"If you have run with the footmen, and they have wearied you, then how can you contend with horses? And if in the land of peace, in which you trusted, they wearied you, then how will you do in the floodplain of the Jordan?" (12:5).

"Your words were found and I ate them, and Your word was to me the joy and rejoicing of my heart; for I am called by Your name, O LORD God of hosts" (15:16).

"Blessed is the man who trusts in the LORD, and whose hope is in the LORD. For he shall be like a tree planted by the waters, which spreads out its roots by the river, and will not fear when heat comes; but its leaf will be green. And will not be anxious in the year of drought, nor will cease from yielding fruit" (17:7–8).

"The heart is deceitful above all things, and desperately wicked; who can know it?" (17:9).

"Then I said, 'I will not make mention of Him, nor speak anymore in His name.' But His word was in my heart like a burning fire shut up in my bones; I was weary of holding it back, and I could not" (20:9).

"For I know the thoughts that I think toward you, says the LORD, thoughts of peace and not of evil, to give you a future and a hope" (29:11).

"And you will seek Me and find Me when you search for Me with all your heart" (29:13).

"Behold, I am the LORD, the God of all flesh. Is there anything too hard for Me?" (32:27).

"Call to Me, and I will answer you, and show you great and mighty things, which you do not know" (33:3).

"This I recall to my mind, therefore I have hope. Through the LORD's mercies, we are not consumed, because His compassions fail not. They are new every morning; great is Your faithfulness" (Lamentations 3:21–23).

Chapter Eleven

Daniel

A Mentally Healthy Man

With twenty million major depressives, fifteen million alcoholics, ten million emotionally disturbed children, five million antisocial personalities, five million psychotics, and over one million drug addicts in this country, one might wonder if mental health ever existed. It did, and it does. You need look no further than the story of Daniel, the celebrated prophet of the Babylonian court. He is one of the most extraordinary examples of mental health in the Bible. The life of Daniel reveals several significant insights into the characteristics of mental health—characteristics that we can apply to our lives today.

Daniel was only sixteen years old when Babylon captured Judah. Scripture states that he had "exceptional qualities" (Daniel 6:3 NIV). He was intelligent, quick to learn, and socially poised; and he was an excellent physical specimen. Because Daniel was such a gifted young man, Nebuchadnezzar chose to train him to occupy a position of administration and authority in the Babylonian kingdom.

Daniel 6:1–5 (NIV) records the following:

> It pleased Darius to appoint 120 satraps to rule throughout the kingdom, with three administrators over them, one of whom was Daniel. The satraps were made accountable to them, so that the king might not suffer loss. Now Daniel so distinguished himself among the administrators and the satraps by his exceptional qualities that the king planned to appoint him over the whole kingdom. At this, the administrators

and the satraps tried to find grounds for charges against Daniel in his conduct of government affairs, but they were unable to do so. They could find no corruption in him, because he was trustworthy and neither corrupt nor negligent. Finally these men said, "We will never find any basis for charges against this man Daniel unless it has something to do with the law of his God."

Every now and then in life, most of us will come across someone who is truly gifted in several areas. On occasion we may encounter someone we want to emulate. Daniel is such a man. You may recall an old song that suggests that we dare to be a Daniel. He certainly sounds worth emulating, doesn't he?

Ezekiel made special mention of Daniel as a righteous man, along with Noah and Job. This was a great honor, considering that Daniel was Ezekiel's contemporary. If most of us were giving a talk today on godly men, we would most likely draw our characters from the past, not from the present. Christ referred to Daniel in Matthew 24:15. Hebrews 11 also alludes to this prophet in the list of great heroes of faith, pointing to the fact that his faith "stopped the mouths of lions" (Hebrews 11:33).

Very little is known of Daniel's first sixteen years, but he must have come from an unusually stable family background. God used those early years to build a man of incredible mental strength, as the following ten characteristics of mental health illustrate.

Ten Characteristics of Mental Health in Daniel's Life

As we consider these characteristics of today's mentally healthy man or woman, it is remarkable to see how clearly they show up in the life of this Old Testament prophet.

An Ability to Withstand Change

The mentally healthy individual can react appropriately to stress. He or she demonstrates both discipline and emotional control, can accept what is unchangeable, and is free from excessive and prolonged anxiety or depression in the face of change. As we grow in Christ, we can withstand more stress than usual, but we need to understand that all of us have limits.

As noted earlier, two psychologists named Holmes and Rahe developed a stress test in 1973 that assigned a certain number of stress units (or points) to different life changes:

Stress Chart

Life Change	Units
Death of a spouse	100
Divorce	73
Marital separation	65
Jail term	63
Death of close family member	63
Personal injury or illness	53
Marriage	50
Fired at work	47
Marital reconciliation	45
Retirement	45
Change in health of family member	44
Pregnancy	40
Sex difficulties	39
Gain of new family member	39
Business readjustment	39
Change in financial state	38
Death of close friend	37
Change to different line of work	36
Change in number of arguments with spouse	35
Mortgage or loan over $10,000	31
Foreclosure of mortgage or loan	30

Stress Chart, continued

Life Change	Units
Change in responsibilities at work	29
Son or daughter leaving home	29
Trouble with in-laws	29
Outstanding personal achievement	28
Wife begins or stops work	26
Begin or end school	26
Change in living conditions	25
Revision of personal habits	24
Trouble with boss	23
Change in work hours or conditions	20
Change in residence	20
Change in schools	20
Change in recreation	19
Change in church activities	19
Change in social activities	18
Mortgage or loan less than $10,000	17
Change in sleeping habits	16
Change in number of family get-togethers	15
Change in eating habits	15
Vacation	13
Christmas	12
Minor violations of the law	11[1]

Researchers have found that an accumulation of two hundred or more life-change units in a single year is usually followed by a significant increase in physical or psychiatric disorders. Recently a young man sat in Frank Minirth's office and related that he could not understand why he was depressed. He had gone through a number of life changes in the past year. In fact, when Frank had him add up the total number of life change units, he came up with more than four hundred.

As Daniel 6 opens, the prophet is about eighty years old. Over the years he had faced unbelievable change. He had been removed from his country at a young age, never to see many of his relatives or friends again. He was taken to a new home, a new school, and a new social situation. On a stress test, he would have had enough points to develop an emotional disorder, but he withstood the changes well.

How many changes have you had in the past year? How many points would you score on the Holmes and Rahe stress test? How have you handled them?

The Ability to Function at Full Capacity— Physically, Intellectually, and Emotionally

Probably the most practical criterion of mental health is how an individual is functioning physically, intellectually, and emotionally. In fact, clinical professionals used to employ the term *neurosis* (a term no longer in common use in psychiatry) to describe individuals who were "not functioning adequately physically, intellectually, and emotionally over an extended period of time." Today the mental health of many individuals has been impaired because of worry, anxiety, depression, or mental confusion.

Daniel excelled physically, intellectually, and emotionally throughout his life. As a youth, he excelled during particularly trying times; and he continued to excel for over eighty years under three different foreign kings. His composure when confronted with the handwriting on the wall (Daniel 5:13–29) was nothing short of remarkable.

At what level are you functioning physically, intellectually, and emotionally?

A Good Attitude: Optimistic, Confident, and Secure

A mentally healthy individual has a good attitude. He or she is basically secure and reflects this with confidence, optimism, and a sense of humor.

Daniel had confidence because of his faith in God. As a youth, he was confident God could make him physically strong even though he refused the king's food. He was confident that, with God's help, he could interpret King Nebuchadnezzar's dream (2:24–45). This same confidence was evident when Daniel interpreted the handwriting on the wall and told King Belshazzar of impending judgment (5:13–29). His confidence was apparent to a third king, Darius, who wanted to put Daniel in charge of his entire kingdom (6:1–3).

Do you have a good attitude? Do you reflect a spirit of confidence with God's help?

An Unwavering Purpose in Life

One of the major determinants that keeps a person on a mentally stable path is an unwavering purpose in life. A pamphlet in the reception room at the Minirth Clinic points out that a person is born, grows up, goes to school, gets a job, marries, and eventually dies; then it asks, Is this all there is to life? The purpose of this question is to make people think about what their real purpose in life is, to ask what is of lasting importance.

Daniel had an ingrained, unwavering purpose in life. He had an eternal perspective. He lived for God and his principles. His brain was programmed through and through with an unwavering desire to do God's will. This is clear from Daniel's earliest days in Babylon, when he purposed not to violate his conscience by eating or drinking the provision of the Chaldeans (1:8). This purpose gave him contentment, happiness, inner peace, and mental stability.

What is your purpose in life?

The Ability to Relate to Others and Build Relationships

When determining the mental health of people who come to his office, Frank often takes special note of how they relate to others (spouse, friends, employer, and so on). A mentally healthy person relates well to a variety of people, and especially to those with whom he or she is in close contact.

Daniel related well to people as a youth, at a time of life when many are too rebellious to deal effectively with people. He demonstrated this same ability as an older man, a time when many have become too set in their ways to accommodate the give-and-take of human relationships, as he "went about the king's business" (8:27). Daniel even related well to a foreign people and was able to work productively with them despite their many cultural and religious differences.

How well do you do in relating to the variety of people in your life?

Balance in Several Important Areas

A balanced life is one of the best indications of mental health. Every person needs a balance between being dependent and independent, between being organized and spontaneous and creative. This balance is especially important in the spiritual areas of a person's life.

Daniel maintained a balance between being dependent and independent. As a youth, he often had to depend on various foreign people who were in positions of authority over him. Yet he could be independent when needed, and he knew how to appeal to his captors successfully in matters of personal conscience and conviction (1:8–9). Although he had been trained in foreign schools, he was never brainwashed as the Chaldean officials had hoped he would be. He could be open and flexible when needed (an important aspect of mental health), but he knew where to draw the line to maintain his independence.

Daniel must also have had a balance between being organized and spontaneously creative. Taken to its extreme, organization can be an obsessive-compulsive personality trait, whereas creativity in its extreme can be a hysterical trait. A highly efficient and effective person needs to have a healthy balance of both.

Daniel maintained a balance in his spiritual life as well. Earlier we noted his emphasis on the Word of God. In Daniel 10:12 (KJV) the emphasis is on prayer: "Then said he unto me, Fear not, Daniel: for from the first day that thou didst set thine heart to understand, and to chasten thyself before thy God, thy words were heard, and I am come for thy words." In Daniel 12:3 (KJV) the emphasis is on witnessing and the promise of salvation: "And they that be wise shall shine as the brightness of the firmament; and they that turn many to righteousness as the stars for ever and ever."

Spiritual balance is one sure indication of mental health in a Christian. Churches that overemphasize doctrine may often seem cold; those that overemphasize witnessing may offend others unnecessarily. Certainly, balance is needed. Daniel had such a balance.

How balanced are you? Are you compulsive in your need to be organized? Are you so spontaneously creative that you have difficulty following through on a task?

Dependable

Another mark of mental health and maturity is dependability. If we were to ask employers what aspect of mental health they look for the most in employees, the majority would probably identify dependability.

Daniel was outstanding in demonstrating dependability and trustworthiness. The presidents and princes of the land where he had been carried captive could find no fault with him, even though they were eager to find some area of corruption or negligence in order to have him removed from office (6:4, 5). This is remarkable when we consider the hundreds of people who must have worked under him. Daniel had strong internal standards that made him dependable. Because of these, he could resist social and environmental pressure; he could withstand the temptation to sin; he could avoid being impulsive. He could be trusted to fulfill his responsibilities.

How dependable are you?

Other-Centered, Not Self-Centered

Another benchmark of mental health is that a person tends to be other-centered rather than self-centered. One who is all wrapped up in his or her own selfish desires, angers, jealousies, suspicions, and problems has very little to give to others and is not showing emotional maturity.

Daniel was other-centered. Although the presidents and princes were jealous of him, there is no indication that Daniel showed vindictiveness toward these wise men. In fact, he even intervened to save their lives when an earlier ruler decreed that all wise men be put to death in view of their inability to tell the king what he had dreamed (2:1–24). He was other-centered. He had enough emotional strength left over after dealing with his own problems to give to others.

How much time do you spend thinking about you and your needs versus thinking about others and their needs?

A Man of the Word

The authors of this book believe that a major indication that a Christian is mentally healthy is whether or not he or she spends time in the Word of God daily. In fact, being in the Word regularly is not only an indication of mental health, the authors believe; it is the ultimate key to mental health for Christians. Jesus once told a group of people that they erred on a particular issue because they knew neither the Word nor the power of God (Matthew 22:29).

People often suffer great emotional pain because they do not make use of the comfort and solace to be found in the pages of Scripture. The Holy Spirit uses the Word of God to produce peace, joy, contentment, and every other vital aspect of mental health. The Word works to counter anxiety, depression, defensiveness, immaturity, and all those traits that generally indicate a lack of mental health.

Several years ago a colleague of Frank's administered a series of psychological tests to a group of Christians to determine if time spent with the Word of God made any difference in their maturity level. He initially divided the group into those who had been Christians for more than three years and those who had been Christians for a shorter period. In general, there was no difference in maturity levels. Next, he divided the group according to those who spent time daily in the Word, those who spent time in the Word a few times a week, and those who hardly ever spent time in the Word. The maturity level was found to be consistently and proportionately related to time spent in the Word. He found that the group that spent time daily in the Word was more mature, more mentally healthy, and showed no significant emotional pathology.

Daniel was a man of God's Word. He greatly valued "the law of his God" (6:5). This was the key to his mental stability; and that stability was reflected in his extreme courage in facing lions, foreign kings, and people who were jealous of him.

How often do you read and enjoy the Bible?

An Acceptance of God as Our Primary Support System

Skeptics have accused Christians of using God as a crutch. Mental health involves realizing that we all have dependency needs, then meeting those needs in healthy ways. God wants us to let him be our primary support system. He longs to be close to us and to meet our needs.

Consider the words that the Lord spoke to the children of Israel:

I remember you,
The kindness of your youth,
The love of your betrothal,
When you went after Me in the wilderness,
In a land not sown.
                    —Jeremiah 2:2

These words sound as if God were reflecting on a pleasant memory. This verse reminds us that God has emotions too. He longs to be close to us. He longs to love us, forgive us, and encourage us. He wants to be our primary support system. To have him as our primary support system is a sign of mental health.

Twice, Daniel watched his world crumble around him, first as he was taken from his homeland to Babylon, and then later as the Medes killed Belshazzar and took over his kingdom (5:30, 31). His external support system fell apart. But Daniel remained mentally healthy because God was his support system, and that was a system that could never fail.

Where does God fit in your support system?

Recommendations for Good Mental Health

For good mental health, the authors of this book recommend considering the following choices:

Avoid intentionally placing yourself in situations that might subject you to too much change and too much stress.

Work on building an adequate self-concept. See yourself realistically. Realistically accept the gifts and abilities God has given you. Accept that because Christ died for you, you are a worthy person.

Do a good job at work. Function in such a manner that you feel competent. Set goals and reach them. However, be careful not to set unrealistic goals that will leave you with a feeling of incompetence if you do not attain them. Each of us needs to develop a place in life where we feel secure and where we function successfully within our abilities.

Develop an unwavering purpose in life. Devote your life to Christ and his goals.

Build a strong support system of close friends around you. Spend time with these friends. Help them, and let them help you. Encourage them. Be happy when they succeed. Share your burdens with your friends.

Work on having a balanced life. Avoid extremes. Learn Bible doctrine, but be sure to work on your prayer life. Work, but also play. Think, but also be sure to learn to feel. Be serious, but learn to laugh. Develop your sense of humor. Laughing relieves as much tension as crying. Enjoying yourself is not a sin. Work on balance in every area of life.

Be dependable. When you demonstrate dependability, you will feel good about yourself—and others will too!

Be other-centered, not self-centered. Get your mind off your own problems. Determine to help someone else this week—either spiritually, psychologically, or physically. By so doing, you will become more objective in dealing with your own problems. Work on being loving, gentle, and forgiving with others.

Learn to love and enjoy the Word of God. Nothing builds us up like the Bible. The Apostle Paul said, "And now, brethren, I commend you to God, and to the word of His grace, which is able to build you up and give you an inheritance among all those who are sanctified" (Acts 20:32 KJV). Make Scripture central in your life. Don't be afraid of God's Word. It will both correct and build you up.

Avoid sin. Sin destroys mental health. The Apostle Peter said that we should avoid fleshly lusts, which war against the soul (1 Peter 2:11). Sin produces sick minds, fluctuating emotions, and weak wills.

Accept God as your primary support system. Realize that if you have accepted Christ, you belong to God. You have a support system that can never fail. You will face trouble in life. There will be ups and downs. Christ said, "Therefore whoever hears these sayings of Mine, and does them, I will liken him to a wise man who built his house on the rock: and the rain descended, the floods came, and the winds blew and beat on the house; and it did not fall, for it was founded on the rock" (Matthew 7:24, 25). With God as our support system, we can stand firm when the winds blow and the rains come. We will be like a tree planted by "the rivers of water" (Psalm 1:2, 3). With God's help, a Christian can develop an attitude of acceptance and an ability to adjust and cope.

The quiz in Exhibit 11.1 is not meant to be a standardized measure of your mental health. However, if you answer the questions carefully and honestly, it will provide clues to evaluating your spiritual and mental health.

Exhibit 11.1.   A Profile of Spiritual Mental Health

Directions
Complete the following profile by circling the letter of the answers that apply to you.

1. Do you read and apply the Word of God to your life?

   (a) Each day   (b) Three times weekly   (c) Seldom

2. During periods of situational stress and rapid change in your life, do you experience difficulty functioning (biologically in terms of sleep disturbance, appetite change, headaches, nervous stomach, decreased sexual interest; or socially resulting in a loss of motivation or interest in work and other daily activities)?

   (a) Seldom   (b) Occasionally   (c) Each day

3. Would your employer say that you are a dependable person?

   (a) Almost always   (b) Usually   (c) Occasionally

Exhibit 11.1.   A Profile of Spiritual Mental Health, *continued*

4. Do you have a tendency to go to extremes in various areas of your life (physical exercise, church work, job, and so on)?

    (a) Seldom   (b) Occasionally   (c) Frequently

5. As a Christian committed to living for God and by his principles, how often do you stop to consider and review your purpose in life?

    (a) Daily   (b) Three times weekly   (c) Seldom

6. Do your thoughts revolve around yourself and your problems, as opposed to focusing on helping others?

    (a) Occasionally   (b) Often   (c) Usually

7. Would your spouse or closest friend say that you have a good attitude?

    (a) Almost always   (b) Usually   (c) Occasionally

8. Do you have close and intimate friends with whom you can share your most private thoughts with confidence that they will accept you?

    (a) Several   (b) A few   (c) None

9. Do you have a primary support system?

    (a) Yes, God   (b) Yes, the family   (c) No
                            (personal or Christian)

10. In how many major areas of life (church, family, job, and so on) do you function well?

    (a) Four or more   (b) Three   (c) Two or less

Scoring
Score one point for each (a) answer, three points for each (b) answer, and five points for each (c) answer.

Evaluation
10–20 = excellent; 21–29 = good; 30 or more = fair.

🌿 Daniel 🌿

Take-Away Messages from the Past

1. Mental health is possible. Daniel had it.
2. The book of Daniel has some wonderful verses for us to study and reflect on.
3. Daniel was an individual of remarkable balance in both his personal and his professional life.

Choices for Today

1. Daniel's life detailed many aspects of mental health. Which three characteristics would you want to give the most attention to in your own life?
2. How is your mental health? What choices that you face fit with those Daniel made? Which of his choices have helped you the most?
3. Which of the Bible verses listed here do you feel would help you? Would you be willing to memorize it this month?

> "Then this Daniel was preferred above the presidents and princes, because an excellent spirit was in him; and the king thought to set him over the whole realm. Then the presidents and princes sought to find occasion against Daniel concerning the kingdom; but they could find none occasion nor fault; forasmuch as he was faithful, neither was there any error or fault found in him" (Daniel 6:3, 4 KJV).

> "Then said he unto me, Fear not, Daniel: for from the first day that thou didst set thine heart to understand, and to chasten thyself before thy God, thy words were heard, and I am come for thy words" (10:12 KJV).

> "And they that be wise shall shine as the brightness of the firmament; and they that turn many to righteousness as the stars for ever and ever" (12:3 KJV).

"And all the inhabitants of the earth are reputed as nothing: and he doeth according to his will in the army of heaven, and among the inhabitants of the earth: and none can stay his hand, or say unto him, What doest thou?" (4:35 KJV).

Chapter Twelve

John the Baptist

A Man Out of Step with Society

Do you sometimes feel like a misfit, misunderstood, even out of step with society? Although we never want to deliberately act weird just for the sake of being different, we need to realize that God has made each of us unique individuals. No matter what your personality type, God has plans for your life.

No one in Scripture better illustrates this fact than John the Baptist. When we look closely at him or try to pinpoint his personality type, we have to admit that he doesn't seem like the kind of person most of us would want to be. If he were alive today, he'd probably be branded as eccentric, if not worse.

Luke 1 records that John was born to an elderly couple by the name of Zacharias and Elizabeth. While Zacharias had been completing his duties as a priest in the temple at Jerusalem, the angel Gabriel appeared to him with the announcement that Elizabeth would have a son, whom they were to call John. Gabriel accompanied this news with the additional assurance that this child would possess the nature of Elijah and turn the hearts of the children of Israel back to the Lord.

Because both Zacharias and Elizabeth were well beyond the childbearing age and Elizabeth had been barren all her life, Zacharias was understandably doubtful. Because of his lack of faith, the Lord caused him to be unable to speak until John's birth (Luke 1:18–20, 64).

After Mary had received a message from Gabriel concerning her own conception, she went to visit Elizabeth, who was also a relative. When she entered the house, Elizabeth heard her greeting and felt the child in her own womb leap. After John was born, Zacharias was once again able to speak; and all the people who lived in the area wondered, "What kind of child will this be?" (1:66).

Scripture mentions nothing about John from the time of his birth until he appeared in the area of the Jordan. Considering their advanced age, his parents may have died while John was still a young boy. In any event, he became a recluse who lived in the desert wilderness of southern Judea. His clothing of camel hair and diet of locusts were certainly eccentric (Matthew 3:4), and he wasn't at all interested in being accepted by the society of his day (3:7–9). He was not diplomatic in his speech and never seemed to care about saying the right thing, an outspokenness that ultimately cost him his life (14:1–12; Mark 6:14–28.).

When he began his ministry, John was unaffected by the crowds that came seeking him. He admitted that he wasn't the messiah or even the reincarnation of Elijah, as some proposed. Instead he characterized himself as "the voice of one crying in the wilderness" (John 1:23).

In a short time, John the Baptist offended Herod by calling his marriage to Herodias, who had previously been married to Philip, Herod's brother, a sin. Herod had John imprisoned and eventually beheaded (Matthew 14:1–12).

Eccentric or Misguided?

The world has no shortage of eccentrics. Some years ago Billy Graham noted that it's estimated that more than two thousand people in the United States claim to be Christ.[1] Most of these are harmless individuals suffering from schizophrenia or some other mental illness. A few, however, have misguided a multitude of people and brought about death and destruction: Jim Jones led over nine hundred followers from the People's Temple to their death at Jonestown; and David Koresh was instrumental in the death of seventy-four of his followers, including twenty-one children, at a Branch Davidian compound near Waco, Texas.

So what separated John from those who misguide and abuse their followers? After John's death Jesus characterized him as the greatest man born of woman (Matthew 11:11). The secret to John's greatness was his attitude toward Christ. He declared in John 3:30, "He must increase, but I must decrease." His focus was on magnifying Jesus. This gave him the freedom to accept his uniqueness as part of God's plan and released him from being concerned about what others thought of him.

Invariably, those who misuse their authority focus on their own gain and glory. A true servant of God doesn't draw attention to himself but echoes with John, "Behold the Lamb of God who takes away the sin of the world!" (John 1:29).

Lessons from John the Baptist

Despite his eccentricities, John's devotion to Christ makes him an excellent subject for study and a source of numerous practical insights and lessons for living the Christian life today. Let's consider several of them.

Popularity Is Fleeting

John experienced tremendous popularity early in his ministry. Without the benefit of any miraculous signs such as those that accompanied Jesus' ministry, John still drew phenomenal crowds. Mark 1:5 says, "Then all the land of Judea, and those from Jerusalem, went out to him and were all baptized by him in the Jordan River, confessing their sins." Even Herod enjoyed listening to this unusual orator (6:20).

Yet it is worth noting that when John was arrested, no one made an effort to secure his release. Although it's true that John's archnemesis, Herodias, had the king's ear, Herod also feared the people; under the right circumstances, he might possibly have been persuaded to banish this popular preacher instead of executing him. But no one made the effort to change John the Baptist's sentence.

Winston Churchill knew that public favor was no proof of real success. Once, after Churchill gave a speech before ten thousand people, a friend asked whether he was impressed that so many had come to hear him speak. Churchill replied, "Not really. A hundred thousand would come to see me hang."[2]

How quickly people will sacrifice their families, their friends, and even their Christian witness for a moment of popularity. But as we can see from the life of John the Baptist, fame has no lasting effect. Those who hang on your every word today will turn their backs on you tomorrow.

How important is popularity to you? What would you be willing to sacrifice to gain it?

Truth Is Dangerous

Despite having spent his formative years in the wilderness, John the Baptist was very aware of what was going on in the cities around him. Current events had not passed him by. He knew that Herod had taken his brother Philip's wife. He even rebuked this wicked king for "all the evils which [he] had done" (Luke 3:19), which seems to indicate that John knew a lot of what Herod was up to. Furthermore, John knew that Herod's tax gatherers were prone to collect more than their due and that his soldiers had a tendency to abuse their power (3:12–14). John also had an amazing ability to cut to the quick of things. And what he offered up was the unvarnished truth.

This faithfulness to the truth resulted in John's arrest, imprisonment, and ultimate execution. Would John have done it all over again, knowing the results? Undoubtedly, yes. John was dedicated to his life's mission of preparing the way for the Messiah (John 1:19–27). This purpose required that he confront people with their sin, and nothing short of the truth would accomplish this goal (Matthew 3:7–12). Truth was not optional with John; it was essential.

Are you willing to tell the truth even if it causes problems for you?

Integrity Is Key to Ministry

John the Baptist had few material possessions, but he had integrity. He lived what he preached and preached what he lived. John was not motivated by material gain. He didn't have a Rolls Royce parked in some hidden spot in the desert or a thick stock portfolio lying on his desk in a plush office as he urged others to give to the poor and the needy (Luke 3:11). John's walk was consistent with his talk.

In the early days of jet aviation, Boeing and Douglas Aircraft were competing for sales to Eastern Airlines, which was headed by famed aviator Eddie Rickenbacker. Rickenbacker told Donald Douglas, founder of McDonnell Douglas, that his company's specifications for the DC-8 were close to Boeing's in everything but noise suppression. Then he gave Douglas a last chance to promise more than the competition. After consulting his engineers, Douglas told Rickenbacker he could not do it. Rickenbacker replied, "I know you can't. I wanted to see if you were still honest. You just got yourself an order worth $135 million. Now go home and silence those jets!"[3]

How important is integrity to you? Do you walk the talk?

Prayer Changes Things

Many of you may have seen this slogan on a plaque perhaps hanging in your mother's home: prayer changes things. Whether it hung in John's home or not, he certainly believed it. Although Scripture never records this eccentric prophet speaking a prayer, yet we know that he was a man of prayer. In fact, he was such a man of prayer that when the disciples came to ask Jesus to teach them to pray, they said, "Lord, teach us to pray as John also taught his disciples" (Luke 11:1).

Jesus' disciples, some of whom had originally been followers of John the Baptist, knew what a prayer warrior this man was. And they wanted to be just like him in that respect.

Furthermore, John not only prayed, he taught others to pray. Although to a certain degree prayer is instinctive (after all, most of us are pretty good at asking for things), we have much to learn about what's appropriate, what's pleasing to God, and what's important in prayer. Whether we use the ACTS prayer acronym (for adoration, confession, thanksgiving, and supplication) or some method of our own making, prayer is something that we not only can practice ourselves but teach to others.

Have you taught your children to pray? Would you know how if you needed to? Is there a new convert in your sphere of influence who could use some instruction in prayer?

Good People Can Doubt

Doubt can plague any one of us. Missionary Gracia Burnham, who was held captive by terrorists in the Philippines for more than a year and whose husband, Martin, was killed during the rescue, writes: "Sometimes I wonder, *Why did Martin die when everyone was praying he wouldn't? Why does Scripture lead you to believe that if you pray a certain way, you'll get what you pray for?* People all over the world were praying that we'd both get out alive, but we didn't."[4] Her questions made her realize that comprehending God's nature isn't always easy.

John the Baptist also had his moments of doubt. Luke 7:19–23 records:

And John, calling two of his disciples to him, sent them to Jesus, saying, "Are You the Coming One, or do we look for another?" When the men had come to Him, they said, "John the Baptist has sent us to You, saying, 'Are You the Coming One, or do we look for another?'" And that very hour He cured many of infirmities, afflictions, and evil spirits; and to many blind He gave sight. Jesus answered and said to them, "Go and tell John the things you have seen and heard: that the blind see, the lame walk, the lepers are cleansed, the deaf hear, the dead are raised, the poor have the gospel preached to them. And blessed is he who is not offended because of Me."

Keep in mind that there's a difference between unbelief and doubt. Henry Drummond, a nineteenth-century preacher and author, wrote, "Christ never failed to distinguish between doubt and unbelief. Doubt is can't believe; unbelief is won't believe. Doubt is honesty; unbelief is obstinacy. Doubt is looking for light; unbelief is content with darkness."[5]

John showed us what to do with do with our legitimate doubts; he began by going directly to the source. He didn't send out his disciples to take a survey to find out what others thought; he didn't try to puzzle it out for himself. Instead, he went directly to Jesus. And so should you. God is not offended by your doubts. Take them before the Lord and admit you have questions.

Then let God's deeds speak for themselves. Jesus told John's disciples to go back and tell him "the things you have seen and heard" (Luke 7:22).

Although seeing miraculous healings and hearing wonderful truths is exciting, we have an even greater proof—the empty tomb. If you can find an explanation for the empty tomb, there may be grounds for doubt. But all the scoffers' explanations fall flat before the empty tomb's witness. If Jesus' body, dead or alive, had been anywhere around, the religious leaders of his day would have produced it and put an end to all this nonsense. But they didn't because they couldn't. It wasn't anywhere to be found.

So what do you do when you have doubts? Do you take them before the Lord? Let him point you to the empty tomb.

What About Us?

So what about us? Challenging, isn't it, as we consider John— politically incorrect, unconcerned about fashion, following an eccentric diet, socially different, not diplomatic, confrontational, refusing others' admiration, paying the ultimate price? Yet his life counted greatly for Christ, and ours can too—no matter what type of personality we have, or how out of step with others we may seem.

🦋 John the Baptist 🦋

Take-Away Messages from the Past

1. For Christ's cause, John was
   ___ Politically incorrect
   ___ Eccentric with dress
   ___ Eccentric in diet
   ___ Socially different
   ___ Not diplomatic
   ___ Confrontational
   ___ Refusing others' admiration
   ___ Willing to pay the ultimate price

2. John's focus was not on himself but rather on magnifying Christ.

3. John knew what to do with his doubts.

Choices for Today

1. Place a check mark by any list item under "Take-Away Messages from the Past" that applies to you because of a stand you took for Christ.

2. What is one choice you could make that would allow you to magnify Christ more?

3. How will you respond when you experience doubts? Will you take them to the Lord, as John did?

Chapter Thirteen

Martha

Focused on Performance

Quick now, off the top of your head, who is the woman in Scripture with whom today's busy twenty-first century woman identifies?

If you replied, "Martha," you might be right. Time after time when Don Hawkins has spoken about Martha or mentioned her on the radio, women have come up to him and said, "I'm such a Martha." His wife, Kathy, frequently speaks to women's groups on the topic of the Martha complex, and she reports the same response. On the other hand, Don can't remember a time when anyone ever said to him, "I'm so much like Mary"—or for that matter, Ruth or Esther or the mother of Jesus or even Lydia. Martha seems to have a corner on the market.

Even though the common denominator for most of these women who identify with Martha includes high stress, perfectionism, many distractions, and frustration with an intense, busy schedule—feeling overworked and underappreciated—Don has found that many of these women seem to wear their Martha identification as a badge of courage. Sometimes he senses a subtle pride in their saying, "You know, I'm a lot like Martha." The implication is "I'm a performance person. I get things done. I don't just sit around thinking and talking. I'm productive."

Personality Label

We live in a time when everybody seems focused on labels, and our personality types are no exception. We may be dominant, influential, steady, or compliant based on the DISC approach;[1] or we could be extroverted or introverted, sensing or intuitive, thinking or feeling, or even judging or perceiving, based on the Myers-Briggs type indicator.[2] We could be one of the four basic temperaments that Hippocrates identified, supposedly based on bodily fluids: sanguine, choleric, melancholy, or phlegmatic.[3] We could be categorized by our friends Gary Smalley and John Trent's animal-based temperament categories, allegedly written on a napkin at 2:00 A.M. one morning in a Denny's restaurant: the take-charge lion; the fun-loving otter; the detail-oriented beaver; or the steady, loyal golden retriever.[4]

Finally, there is the type A–type B categorization developed by Friedman and Rosenman.[5] Without question many of us, male and female, find the highly productive type A label something we are pleased to wear. Had she lived in our day, perhaps Martha would have too.

The problem is that the type A (perfectionist, obsessive-compulsive, or whatever label we choose to use) person faces significant road hazards. For example, type A individuals tend to be conscientious, dutiful, highly motivated, hardworking, and possessed with a strict conscience. As one diligent type A person frequently told his children, "Work makes life sweet." Yet although type A individuals can be productive and successful, they frequently burn out. They expect a great deal of themselves (no perfectionist has ever achieved perfection), and they become intensely angry when they or others demonstrate such imperfections as losing the car keys, misplacing a checkbook or ATM card, or even failing to keep the checkbook balanced. These perfectionistic traits can create conflict and chaos in marriage and work relationships.

Let's Meet Martha

With these personality traits in mind, let's meet Martha and her family. We'll begin in Luke 10. Jesus had already predicted his impending death in Jerusalem (9:44), appointed seventy additional followers to carry his message throughout Israel (10:1), and continued to instruct his inner circle of twelve disciples (vv. 23–24). When confronted by a religious lawyer, he elaborated on the twofold obligation of the great commandment: love God wholeheartedly and love your neighbor unconditionally (v. 27). He then illustrated what it means to love your neighbor as yourself by telling the parable of the Good Samaritan, a study in compassion.

Soon thereafter Jesus and his disciples entered the village of Bethany, where a woman named Martha welcomed him into her house.

A few years ago while touring Israel with three busloads of friends on a tour sponsored by Back to the Bible, Don and Kathy Hawkins visited the site of the village where Martha lived in the first century, located on the southeastern slope of the Mount of Olives, approximately two miles southeast of Jerusalem. Today the village is called El Azaryia—apparently in honor of Lazarus, Martha's brother, whom Jesus would raise from the dead.

Gracious hospitality has been a Middle Eastern tradition from time immemorial; and Scripture is filled with examples, beginning with Abraham, of those who entertained strangers. In fact, God had commanded the Israelites, "Love the stranger, for you were strangers in the land of Egypt" (Deuteronomy 10:19). We immediately discover in Luke 10:38 that Martha was an eager and exceptional hostess. She welcomed Jesus into her house; she was busy attending to all the details; and she took an extremely conscientious approach to making Jesus' visit an enjoyable one.

Now let's keep in mind a couple of things that will help us understand what was happening. When you welcomed someone into your home for a visit in Jesus' time, this usually involved not just a meal but an overnight visit—frequently lasting two days. In addition, Jesus was traveling with a number of people: the twelve disciples for certain and probably several women.

Despite the aplomb with which Martha seemed to handle Jesus' arrival, Luke the physician and gospel writer was quick to point out the problems lurking beneath Martha's successful veneer. Let's consider seven of Martha's problems from this portion of Luke and see if we can relate to any or all of them today. Please keep in mind that Marthaism, if we can call it that, is an equal opportunity problem affecting men and women alike.

Focused on Control

The first thing we notice about Martha is that she seemed to want to be in control. Even though we learn from this passage in Luke 10 and others that Mary and Lazarus lived in the same home as their sister, Martha, Luke observed that Martha welcomed Jesus into "her house." Let's not miss the significance and precision of Luke's record. He avoided saying "their house," probably because Martha was the dominant person in the family. Perhaps she had purchased the house using her own resources; maybe she was the eldest daughter and had thus inherited the home—she certainly seemed to exhibit a lot of the traits commonly found in firstborn children. In fact, if Martha had owned a donkey and if she had a bumper sticker on her donkey, it might have read "A woman's place is in control."

For many of us, control—whether of our lives and schedules or of those around us—is an important issue. Martha probably had a number of servants, and she and the servants were working frantically to make sure everything was perfectly in place for the showcase meal she planned to serve Jesus and the other guests. When she found that Mary wasn't helping enough, she decided to take charge of her sister's life, even if it required enlisting Jesus' help.

The drive to seize control of every aspect of our lives—time, schedules, environment, and even those of others—is a strong temptation in our day. Some time ago the employees of a large manufacturing company threw a party in honor of their vice president, Jack. Ironically, they were celebrating Jack's firing. The reason? Jack was a strongly control-oriented micromanager. He insisted on supervising and approving even the simplest decisions, such as which office supplies to purchase and from which vendors. He constantly looked over the shoulders of everyone in middle management, causing great frustration. No wonder everyone was ready to party when Jack was let go.

Perhaps this may be a good time to ask yourself: Would those in my life describe me as a control freak? Do I strive excessively to maintain control over such factors in my life as time and money? How do I handle interruptions? Do I see them as a challenge to my control and sanity or as opportunities to be of greater service to God and others? Like Martha, many of us may need to come to a fuller, more practical recognition that God is sovereign and deserves to be in control—not us.

Task Oriented

Another fact we quickly learn about Martha is that she was task oriented. Now this may not seem like a problem to many of us; but in fact, it's possible to be too extreme when it comes to tasks and responsibilities. Some of us, to be frank about it, are downright lazy and irresponsible. However, that wasn't Mary's problem; the real issue here is that Martha was task oriented to a fault: "Martha was distracted with much serving" (Luke 10:40). The words Luke uses to describe Martha's state of mind are significant. The term *distracted* indicates the idea of something drawn around, as a belt would be drawn around the waist. In fact, Martha felt tied up in knots. After all, she had at least sixteen to feed for dinner—probably more—and one of them was perfect! Just put yourself in her sandals. There was a lot to do, not enough help, and not enough time. The overload she felt must have been overwhelming. No wonder she was far less concerned with sitting at Jesus' feet the way her sister did than checking tasks off her to-do list.

How many of us can relate to this task orientation? How often do we derive more satisfaction from getting things done than from learning, growing, or just being? As Don Hawkins's wife, Kathy, likes to put it, Martha had allowed herself to become a "human doing" instead of a human being. Can you relate?

Highly Competitive

Another problem in Martha's life is that she tended to be highly competitive. Here we discover sibling rivalry rearing its ugly head, even in the presence of the Master. The text reminds us that Martha's sister, Mary, was sitting at Jesus' feet and listening to his Word. Luke used the word *parakathesaisa*, to "sit beside," to describe what Mary was doing, and this is the only time the word appears in the New Testament. It's a term that indicates how very close Mary sat to Jesus and how eagerly she listened to his words.

Scripture doesn't tell us precisely what troubled Martha the most about what her sister was doing. Perhaps she felt left out because of Mary's choice of activity, or possibly she felt shamed and humiliated because Mary, as a woman, was doing something only men did, listening to a rabbi, and in a public setting at that. After all, what would the neighbors think? Martha's primary concern was probably that there was far too much to do, and Mary was simply not pulling her share of the load. That's the impact of what Martha says in 10:40: "Lord, do you not care that my sister has left me to serve alone? Therefore tell her to help me."

Frequently today we may be tempted to fall into the trap of rivalry, sibling or otherwise. Someone else may appear to have fewer responsibilities. Perhaps someone at work receives a greater amount of recognition for doing less work. Rivalry can lead to resentment, which can be spiritually devastating. Remember how strongly Peter rebuked Simon the Sorcerer, who had been called "the great power of God" and had the ability to perform the most dramatic miracles in Samaria until Peter and John arrived on the scene? Peter responded to Simon's request to purchase God's power by labeling his attitude "wickedness" and pointing out "you are poisoned by bitterness and bound by iniquity" (Acts 8:18–23). May we not succumb to the temptation to become competitive with and bitter toward those around us.

However, some of us may need to go back and deal with those unresolved conflicts with family members and siblings from the past. If we need to ask forgiveness, let's not hesitate to do so.

Advice Giver

Not only did Martha want to be in control, achieve all her tasks, and compete successfully with her sister, she also was eager to give advice. On the verge of becoming stressed out with the magnitude of what she had to do, she found herself coping by moving into the imperative mode. Luke's language indicates how suddenly and dramatically she charged into the Lord's presence, accused him of not caring for her dilemma, then instructed him to tell her sister to quit wasting time sitting there listening to the Master and instead get busy helping with all the chores.

Several things about this confrontation are striking. First, Martha's interruption clearly took her from being a gracious hostess to going to the brink of rudeness and beyond. Second, her phrase "Do you not care?" was a very sharp rebuke. Scripture uses *not caring* to contrast the good shepherd who cares for the sheep with the hireling who "does not care about the sheep" (John 10:13) and to describe the attitude of Judas, who didn't care about the poor in his role as treasurer but only about stealing from the disciples' funds (12:6). Martha's was a stinging accusation, directed toward the Lord; and it stands in sharp contrast to the words of John the evangelist, who pointed out, "Now Jesus loved Martha and her sister and Lazarus" (11:5).

Frequently, like Martha, we may be tempted to forget just how much the Lord cares for us. If this happens, go back to read the gospel accounts, just so you'll remember how deeply he cares, how much he sacrificed, and how great was the measure of his love. How tempting it can be when the pressures of life pile up on us to think that the Lord doesn't care and even to accuse him of acting with careless indifference. But he never does. As the author of Hebrews (4:15, 16) points out, "We do not have a High Priest who cannot sympathize with our weaknesses, but was in all points tempted as we are, yet without sin. Let us therefore come boldly to the throne of grace, that we may obtain mercy and find grace to help in time of need."

The ultimate irony of this portion of Scripture is that Martha was presuming to give advice to the omniscient Lord himself: "Tell her to help me!" she ordered the Lord. But this is not the only time Martha presumed to correct Jesus. Remember what happened when Lazarus died? Jesus had delayed his coming to Bethany, even when he heard that his friend was sick. He had taken the time to explain to his disciples that what was happening was designed to strengthen their faith.

Yet when Jesus arrived, Martha's first words were, "Lord, if you had been here, my brother would not have died" (John 11:21). From a positive perspective, her words indicated a level of faith. On the other hand, the rebuke in her words is as obvious as an elephant in a living room: "If you had just come earlier, Lord, this wouldn't have happened. You're late, Jesus!"

Yet before we condemn Martha for this, let's ask ourselves how many times we've demanded in our prayers that the Lord meet certain needs within our time parameters. "Lord, we need these funds for our ministry, and we need them before the tenth of the month." "Lord, there's a lot to be done—we need workers now, not tomorrow." Let's be cautious that our prayers recognize his sovereignty and that we not try to squeeze his timetable to fit our schedule.

A short time later, Martha took it upon herself to instruct the Lord regarding the condition of her brother's body. Jesus stood before the tomb and ordered, "Take away the stone." Martha immediately interrupted, "Lord, by this time there is a stench, for he has been dead four days" (John 11:39). She trusted in Jesus, and she knew he could heal sick people. But she was about to learn that he could raise dead people. How easy it is for us to place the Lord in a box or come to the conclusion that he can do certain things, meet certain needs, but not beyond the limits we, in our finite thinking, place on his power. Did she think Jesus didn't understand the process of decomposition? We smile at the thought of Martha attempting to educate Jesus about these things—after all, as John (1:3) pointed out in the beginning of his gospel, "All things were made through him."

Yet Jesus showed nothing but restraint in the face of Martha's imperious attitude and attempt to give advice and instruction. Whereas we might have been tempted to respond, "Shut up, Martha. Watch what I'm about to do," the Master simply replied, "Did I not say to you that if you would believe you would see the glory of God?" (John 11:40). Then at his urging, they rolled away the stone—and the rest, as they say, is history!

Perhaps some of us need to admit that we spend too much time in the imperative mood, giving advice to others around us, and even trying to tell God how to run his universe. Far better that we learn to receive and respond to the counsel he gives us from his Word and through his Spirit.

Struggling with Anger

When you listen to the tone of Martha's words, you can reach only one conclusion: she was angry. She wasn't simply irritated; she was beyond frustrated; she was, to put it mildly, hacked and frosted.

We think of anger as an emotion that is always wrong. We can only speculate at the tone of Martha's voice, but her words made her feelings clear: "Lord, don't you care that my sister has left me to do the work by myself? Tell her to help me" (Luke 10:40 NIV).

Anger is an emotion that operates like the red warning light on the dashboard of a car. It signals to us that something is wrong, a threat exists, a problem needs to be corrected. From Martha's perspective, the warning light indicated that things weren't going to get done unless Mary decided to quit wasting her time and the Master's and get with the program. Without question, the program was Martha's plan for getting everything done in time for dinner.

We can just imagine the kind of thoughts running through her mind. *What is this lame-brained sister of mine thinking? Why is she sitting there listening to Jesus? Women aren't supposed to do that anyway. Doesn't she remember all the things I told her we needed to do? The pottery needs to be cleaned; the oil lamps set out for the evening meal; the guest room walls dusted*—Martha's list probably went on and on.

Maybe she felt like choking her sister. In any case, her abrupt intervention into the conversation indicated just how angry she felt.

One of the surefire signs of approaching burnout is irritation that boils over into anger. We find ourselves snapping at our spouses, yelling at our children, putting down our fellow workers, or even verbally pounding our pastor. The anger may be a signal that we are overcommitted or that we have misplaced our priorities. Let's not overlook this flashing red light on the dashboard of our lives.

Anxiety and Inner Turmoil

Jesus replied to Martha's tirade by immediately identifying her core problem. She was worried and troubled about many things. The word for worried, *anxious*, comes from a root term, *merizo*, that means "to distract or divide." Of the twenty-five times this word is used in Scripture, five are positive. For example, Paul used the term in 1 Corinthians 12:25 to indicate the kind of appropriate concern we should have for every member of the body of Christ. Then in Philippians 2:20 he identified Timothy as a man who "will sincerely care for your state."

Yet Jesus used this same word five times in Matthew 6:19–34 to warn against the dangers of distracting anxiety; and in Luke 8:14 he pointed out the danger of being "choked with cares, riches, and pleasures of life."

In addition, Jesus used another word to describe Martha's mental state: "troubled." That word comes from the Latin root from which we get the English word *turbulence*. Anyone who's spent much time flying has undoubtedly experienced the unsettling effects of encountering rough, choppy air. Martha's life and mind at this point had become filled with turbocharged turbulence. She felt overwhelmed with distractions.

Anxiety has become one of the major mental health issues of our time. It can range from mild distraction to a crippling mental and emotional state. Sometimes it requires medical treatment.

However, in Martha's case, and frequently in ours, the anxiety within is simply a symptom of a deeper spiritual problem. At this point in Martha's encounter with Jesus, we're about to get a glimpse of her core problem.

Priorities out of Focus

It's impossible to miss the contrast in Jesus' words to Martha: "You are worried and troubled about many things. But one thing is needed, and Mary has chosen that good part, which will not be taken away from her" (10:41, 42). With surgical precision Jesus laid bare the heart of this dear woman and demonstrated the core issue with which she struggled—the same one with which many of us wrestle—misplaced priorities.

"But wait," you protest, "I have so many things I need to do. Read the Bible. Pray. Study. I need to attend church. I need to be involved in Christian service. I need to give. I need to discharge my responsibilities on the building committee or in the nursery. And those are just the things in the realm of my spiritual life and church attendance!"

It's true that we all have many responsibilities, competing demands, and overlapping areas of concern. Martha certainly did, and the Lord wasn't condemning her concern for housework or for getting things in order. He had already weighed in on the side of hospitality when he suggested that anyone who served a cup of cold water in his name wouldn't lose his or her reward. So that was not the issue.

No, the issue for Martha, as for us, involves choosing what's best over what is simply good. It doesn't take a biblical scholar to figure out the meaning of the words *one thing*. Jesus' point seems evident— that the one best thing that should overshadow all other things, including those that might be considered good, involves drawing close to him, listening to him, and being in fellowship with him. Nothing—absolutely nothing—is of greater importance.

In her excellent book *Martha to the Max*, Debi Stack writes this about her own response to this issue: "For about twenty years now, since the peak of my workaholism, I've been sitting and listening. Somewhere along the way, I stopped being obsessed with defining *'one thing'* into a specific task to perform and evaluate. And I also learned this: sitting wasn't the *one thing*, but the *one thing* made Mary sit. Listening wasn't the *one thing* either, but the *one thing* made Mary listen . . . perhaps *one thing* is not the thing to do, but a way to be; not a place to go, but a place to begin."[6] What a profound insight!

For Martha, for Mary, for Debi, and for all of us, the real issue comes down to this question: Have we come to the place where, as Jesus pointed out earlier in Luke 10, we've come to love the Lord with all our heart, all our soul, all our strength, and all our mind? When we have, it won't be reflected in just going through the ritual of devotions or Bible study. We'll be so eager to learn from him that we'll find ourselves sitting close at his feet, listening to him, and growing more like him.

The Master's Perspective

If Jesus were talking to Martha in today's language, how do you think he might have phrased his responses to her? He might have begun with the following sentence: "Martha, you're not paying attention to me."

We draw this inference from the fact that Jesus repeated her name, "Martha, Martha" (10:41). This is one of only seven times in which Scripture repeats a name.[7]

So why did Jesus repeat Martha's name? Perhaps because he wanted to gently rebuke her in a manner consistent with his compassion. But he may have repeated her name for the same reason we often repeat our children's names or the names of those around us: we simply want to get their attention. You see, the last thing on Martha's mind at this point was Jesus himself or what he might have to say to her. She was far too wrapped up in her own performance and responsibilities. Frequently we find ourselves in the same situation. We are so into our own agenda that we're not paying any attention to the Lord. In a twenty-first century world cluttered with competing agendas, messages, and demands, let's not miss the still small voice of the Savior, even if he has to whisper our name twice.

Next he might have said: "Martha, you have too many irons in the fire." That message is implied in Jesus' statement pointing out Martha's worry and agitation over many things. Like the agitator in a washing machine, her stomach was probably churning furiously as she thought about all there was to do. Like many of us, Martha probably had great trouble using the simple word *no* as a tool to weed out some of life's overwhelming demands.

Think about the idea behind the phrase *too many irons in the fire*. Imagine yourself a cowboy or cowgirl attempting to brand calves in the spring. Now, how many branding irons does it take to brand a calf? "Only one," you reply. That's obvious, yet we may have so many irons in our fire that none of them can do an effective job, and we can't use all of them. After all, a cowboy with a branding iron in each hand would never be able to hold a calf down to get the brand in place!

Are there some things in your life you need to say no to, some chores you need to pass along to someone else? Are there things in your life that aren't really bad but are not of lasting value? Maybe it's time to dust off that word *no* and start using it again. Then we'll have time for what Martha needed most.

Finally, Jesus might have said: "Martha, you're neglecting what matters most and is best." The emphasis in the Lord's final words to Martha lies on the words *one thing*. Jesus went on to point out three characteristics of this *one thing*. First, it was needed. It was not an optional item at extra cost, like power steering or power windows on an automobile. No, this was more like the engine, the transmission, or the tires. Second, Jesus identified the part that Mary chose as "that good part" (10:42), something of inherent value, something consistent with God's good character. Finally,

Jesus said, "This will not be taken away from her" (10:42). Its value was lasting.

But it all comes down to a choice. Jesus commended Mary for choosing what was needful, good, and lasting. What had she chosen? The priority of that personal relationship with the Lord as reflected in Jesus' words, "Love the Lord your God with all your heart, with all your soul, with all your strength, and with all your mind" (10:27).

Years ago Don Hawkins attended a seminar taught by management guru Stephen Covey. In that seminar Covey told the story that's also in his book *First Things First*. A college professor began a class lecture with a demonstration. Setting a jar in a pan on the desk before him, he removed a pan of fairly large rocks from behind his desk, then proceeded to fill the jar with the rocks. Then he asked, "How many of you believe this jar is full?"

The class responded with the obvious answer. Every hand went up.

Next the professor removed a pan of gravel from behind his desk and proceeded to pour gravel into the jar around the larger stones. Then he repeated his question, "How many of you now think that this jar is full?"

By now some of the sharper members of the class had begun to catch on. Only half the hands went up this time.

Next the professor repeated his action with a pan of sand, then with a jar of water. Finally he concluded his demonstration by asking, "What's the point of all this anyway?"

To which one of the self-impressed students in the rear of the classroom responded, "If you work hard enough, you can always cram a little bit more into your life."

Shaking his head, the professor responded, "Not at all. The real point is, if you don't start with the big rocks, you'll never get them in."[8]

Think about that story in terms of what Jesus told Martha. If you don't put the one big rock into place first, you'll be distracted by all the other little things.

🌿 Martha 🌿

Take-Away Messages from the Past

1. No matter how desperately we want to be in control, life will ultimately prove to us that we are not.

2. Some things are more important than getting every task completed on time and in an orderly fashion.

3. The Lord never needs our advice, no matter how much we may think he does.

4. Anger is an emotion that seldom leads to a positive and constructive solution.

5. Inner turmoil results from having too much to do and failing to take time to make relationships with God and others a priority.

6. When we fail to make the main thing the main thing, we really can't achieve anything of eternal worth.

Choices for Today

1. What is one specific way you could choose to surrender control to the Lord? After all, he is sovereign.

2. What is one specific way you could choose to make relationships a priority over tasks? People are more important than projects.

3. What is one specific way you could, when tempted to give advice to God or others, choose to double-check to be sure it's what the Lord is leading you to do? If it's advice for him, it is never appropriate.

4. What is one specific way you could choose to turn anger and vengeance over to God? Anger can serve as a signal that we may be overcommitted or have our priorities out of focus.

5. What is one specific way you could choose to "cast all your care upon him" since he cares for us (1 Peter 5:7) and replace anxiety with prayer (Philippians 4:6)?

6. What is one specific way you could choose to make loving the Lord wholeheartedly the most important priority of your life, closely followed by loving your neighbor unconditionally?

Chapter Fourteen

Peter

The Risk Taker

One of the deacons in the first church he pastored told Terry, a friend of Don Hawkins, "Son, you'll never amount to much of anything in the Lord's work. You spend entirely too much time trying to have fun driving fast cars and motorcycles, jumping out of airplanes, and scuba diving. You need to decide whether you want to have fun in life or serve God."

Perhaps this crotchety old deacon's concern with his young pastor was understandable. After all, if the dictionary had a listing for *risk taker,* Terry's picture would probably be there.

From his earliest days in high school, Terry drove fast cars; he was ticketed several times for street racing. While in college, he purchased his first motorcycle, a Harley-Davidson. He took up parasailing, then graduated to parachuting, and became virtually addicted to scuba diving. Yet through all these adrenaline-fueled pursuits, Terry never lost sight of the wonder of his relationship with Christ and his desire to serve his Savior. That's what drove him to complete Bible college and seminary, then become a pastor. In many ways Terry's personality was similar to that of the ultimate biblical risk taker, Simon Peter.

If Peter had lived in our day, he probably would have been into parachuting, hot-air ballooning, skydiving, hang gliding, scuba diving, or some other dangerous and exciting hobby or career. Scripture records that he was the only individual, other than Jesus himself, to walk on water. This Galilean fisherman threw himself into life with a zest for making the most of every situation. Physically and verbally, he illustrates the popular phrase *Go for it!*

But Peter's physical and verbal impulsivity sometimes created problems. When he walked on the water, he was a classic example of faith—as long as he kept his eyes on the Lord. When he took his eyes off Jesus and focused on his surroundings, he started to sink. In a sense that event helps us to understand the significance of what we need to learn from Peter. God can use those exuberant risk takers, like Peter and Terry, only to the degree that they maintain their focus and commitment to Christ and sustain that commitment by steady Christian growth. Otherwise, they are likely to experience significant ups and downs, perhaps even major failures.

Ups and Downs

Peter's life, especially at first, was certainly characterized by ups and downs. For example, when Jesus asked, "Who do men say that I, the Son of Man, am?" (Matthew 16:13), Peter quickly blurted out the correct answer, "You are the Christ, the Son of the living God" (16:16). However, Peter, who according to Jesus had spoken for God, quickly wound up becoming a mouthpiece for Satan. When Jesus began explaining that as Messiah, he must go to Jerusalem and die, Peter immediately began rebuking him, "Not so, Lord." Jesus' response was swift and certain, "Get behind Me, Satan! You are an offense to Me, for you are not mindful of the things of God, but the things of men" (16:23).

Note the use of the words "mindful of" in this verse. The Lord seemed to be pointing out that Peter had not taken time to consider the significance of what he had said. We see this same impulsivity in Peter on the Mount of Transfiguration (Matthew 17) a short while later. Invited along with James and John to catch a preview of Jesus in his glory, Peter was overcome with the emotion of the moment. The text records, "When *Peter answered and said* to Jesus, 'Rabbi, it is good for us to be here; and let us make three

tabernacles: one for you, one for Moses, and one for Elijah'—
because he did not know what to say" (Mark 9:5, 6; emphasis added).

Like many of us, Peter had shifted his tongue into fast forward
while his mind was still in pause mode. His comments certainly
indicate that his heart was in the right place: "It is good for us to be
here; if You wish, let us make here three tabernacles: one for You,
one for Moses, and one for Elijah" (Matthew 17:4). However,
God's pointed response to Peter provides an important lesson for
us: "This is my Son, whom I love, with him I am well pleased. Listen to him!" (v. 5 NIV).

We see another example of Peter's impulsivity when Jesus was
arrested in the Garden of Gethsemane. Peter, James, and John had
fallen asleep after the Master had invited them to watch with him
and pray. When the soldiers arrived to arrest Jesus, Peter swung into
action. Pulling out his dagger, he sliced an ear off one of the high
priest's servants. Because Peter was not a soldier but a fisherman, it's
safe to assume that he failed to hit his intended target, probably the
middle of the servant's head. Miraculously restoring the servant's
ear, Jesus gently chided Peter, "Put your sword in its place, for all
those who take the sword will perish by the sword" (Matthew
26:52).

How encouraging it is to see that Jesus can graciously put right
the things that those who are impulsive by nature foul up. The
Lord doesn't lose patience with impulsive individuals. Instead, he
wants to direct and channel our impulsiveness into creativity, our
energy into effective service. This is precisely what occurred with
the Apostle Peter.

Failure in His Strength

However bold they might try to appear, the strength of impulsive
individuals like Peter frequently fails. That's precisely what occurred on the night of Jesus' arrest and trial. During the course of
the night, three individuals, one a servant girl, confronted Peter

with the fact that he had been one of Jesus' associates. Earlier Jesus had warned, "I tell you, Peter, the rooster shall not crow this day before you will deny three times that you know me" (Luke 22:34). In each instance, just as the Lord had predicted, Peter—brave, bold, and courageous (in his own estimation)—denied any knowledge of the Master. Why did he do this? Undoubtedly, he was frightened at the prospect of his own death. Ironic, is it not, that the man who was willing to pull a sword and fight the soldiers who arrested Jesus and who so frequently affirmed, "You are the Christ" (Matthew 16:16; John 6:69) wound up cowering in terror before a servant girl?

Frequently those of us who are risk takers tend to overestimate ourselves. We may say, "No problem, I can add one more thing to my schedule without any difficulty" or "My friend may succumb to temptation but not me!" or "I'm a pretty shrewd financial analyst. I know this investment is risky, but I have the personality and the savvy to succeed where others fail."

That's exactly what Peter did. Earlier he had stated, "Even if all fall away on account of you, I never will. Even though the rest will" (Matthew 26:33 NIV). Overestimating ourselves often leads to a dramatic failure similar to Peter's. Peter had failed to remember what is so important even to us today, the words of Jesus just a few hours before as he celebrated his final Passover meal with his disciples in a borrowed upper room: "Without Me you can do nothing" (John 15:5b).

In many ways Peter must have been very likable. He was extremely outgoing and personable, and he loved to talk. He never seemed to be at a loss for words. Recognized as a leader among the disciples, he overshadowed his brother Andrew, who brought him to the Lord in the first place. He seemed to enjoy receiving attention, whether from the Lord, the disciples, or others who followed Jesus. Peter was capable of emotional highs and lows: highs such as he experienced at Jesus' transfiguration (Matthew 17:1–8) and at his stirring sermon on the day of Pentecost, when three thousand responded to his invitation to repentance (Acts 2:14–39); and lows, such as the moment when he heard the rooster crow after

Peter had denied knowing Jesus (Luke 22:60–62) and when the Apostle Paul rebuked Peter for no longer eating with Gentile believers in Antioch (Galatians 2:11, 12).

The Lord's Plan for Peter

Peter's life was full of ups and downs. He had a risk-taking mentality and a go-for-it approach to life. Just take a look at how he plunged into the lake of Galilee and swam to shore to meet Jesus (John 21) or demanded that the Lord give him a complete bath rather than wash his feet (John 13). Despite Peter's bold impulsiveness, the Lord had great plans for him. Jesus intended to take this somewhat inconsistent individual and turn him into a man with the stability of a rock. How do we know this? It is evident from Peter's very first encounter with Jesus. Peter's friend John recorded the event in the first chapter of his gospel. It occurred on the day after John the Baptist had publicly recognized Jesus as the Lamb of God who would take away the sin of the world (John 1:29). Andrew, one of two of John's disciples who had begun following Jesus, decided he needed to find his brother Simon (Peter's original name). You can almost hear the exuberance in the words John recorded Andrew as telling him, "We have found the Messiah!" (1:41). And he brought Peter to Jesus.

Given what we know of Peter's boldness and curiosity, it may not seem surprising that he was so quick to follow Andrew. Perhaps his curiosity was aroused, or maybe Andrew just had a special knack for bringing people to the Lord. In any case, the initial encounter was brief. Jesus simply looked at Peter and said, " 'You are Simon the son of Jonah. You shall be called Cephas' [or Peter] (which is translated, A Stone)" (John 1:42). It certainly seems ironic that the name *Peter* means "stone" or "rock," when one would hardly have considered Peter to be a stable individual at that point in his life. Yet Jesus knew what his ultimate plan for this impetuous individual would be; and as the Lord worked on Peter over time, the apostle would increasingly come to live up to that name.

Two things are significant about this encounter. The first is the word John used to describe the fact that Jesus looked at Peter (John 1:42). *Emblepsas* indicates a penetrating gaze. A literal translation might be "He looked right into Peter." Luke (22:61) used the same word to describe the look that Jesus gave Peter after he denied three times that he knew the Master. It's a word that reminds us that the Lord has the ability to see beneath the surface, to penetrate the depths of our hearts and minds. He knows everything there is to know about us; he is aware of our weaknesses; and he fully understands our strengths and our potential. The Lord could see the ups and downs that Peter's road would bring, but he also saw the ultimate potential. Peter would become a solid foundation stone on which Christ's work would be built. Ultimately, even Paul would recognize Peter as a "pillar" in the church (Galatians 2:9).

The second thing about this encounter is that it laid the foundation for Peter's robust faith in the Lord Jesus. None of the gospels goes into detail about Peter's conversion experience. However, Peter described what happened to him and many others who met the Savior: "Blessed be the God and Father of our Lord Jesus Christ, who according to his abundant mercy has begotten us again to a living hope through the resurrection of Jesus Christ from the dead" (1 Peter 1:3).

Peter and the Ultimate Risk

God had reached out to Peter in the person of his Son, the Lord Jesus Christ, whose resurrection guaranteed the new birth that Peter and others had experienced. You see, the ultimate solution for the risk taker's (or anyone else's) greatest problem, is the removal of the ultimate risk—spending eternity separated from God. The only protection from that risk, according to Peter, is the blood of God's precious, spotless Lamb—the Lord Jesus.

The only way any of us can have that risk removed is by admitting that we are sinners in need of a savior and placing our trust in Jesus Christ, who died on a cross to pay for our sins and whose resurrection guarantees salvation of all who place their trust in him. As Peter would later write, he and others who trusted Christ receive an incorruptible, unfading inheritance. And everyone who has trusted Christ is kept by the power of God (1 Peter 1:4, 5). These cardinal facts are not only true for Peter; they apply to believers today as well. No wonder the apostle wrote, "In this you greatly rejoice" (1:6).

Not only did the Lord Jesus provide Peter with both a new name that reflected his ultimate character and a new life that made it possible, he provided this exuberant risk taker with a new mission and purpose in life. Peter and his brother, along with their two fishing partners, James and John, had begun traveling with Jesus around Galilee. They had even sojourned to Jerusalem with him to celebrate Passover. A watershed event occurred after the four fishermen had spent the night plying their trade on the lake of Galilee, with no fish to show for their efforts. As they washed and mended their nets, Jesus arrived, followed by a large crowd. Walking directly to Peter's boat, he interrupted the fisherman and asked him to put out a short distance from the land. From there he began to teach the multitudes. Luke doesn't go into detail as to what the Lord taught or tell us Peter's response. Perhaps Peter felt sleepy after an all-night fishing stand. Luke does tell us, however, that Peter did exactly what the Lord asked.

But the real test began after the Lord finished that day's lesson. He turned to Peter and said, "Launch out into the deep and let down your nets for a catch" (Luke 5:4). Peter's response is understandable: "Master, we have toiled all night and caught nothing." Peter knew that Jesus wasn't a fisherman; furthermore, his years of experience had taught him that nighttime—certainly not deep water in the daytime—provided the best opportunity to catch fish. But Peter didn't hesitate. At this point his impulsivity stood him in good stead, and he took the risk: "Nevertheless, at Your word I will let down the net," he said (5:5).

In doing so Peter illustrated one of the most important principles of Christian living: obedience brings success and blessing; disobedience guarantees disappointment and failure. What if Peter had chosen to say no? What if he had countered the Lord's instruction by trying to explain what he knew about fishing? Sometimes we're tempted to try to impose what we know on the Lord's plan or to tell him and others how his work needs to be done, when all he wants is our simple obedience. He is far more interested in our availability than in our ability.

Notice the result: not just one boatload of fish but two boatloads! So what was Peter's response to this unparalleled success? Did he stand on the prow of his boat and yell to the multitudes, "Look what a great fisherman I am"? No, he didn't even say, "Look what a lucky fisherman I am!"

Instead, he fell on his knees before Jesus, saying, "Depart from me, for I am a sinful man, O Lord!" (Luke 5:8). Now there is a good side and a bad side to Peter's response. Falling before the Lord and acknowledging his sinfulness was the most appropriate thing Peter could do. After all, we are all sinners, and none is saved except by the grace of God. None of us is capable of carrying out works that will please the Lord, apart from the recognition of our own fallibility and unworthiness. But his impulsive request, "Depart from me," was not what the Lord wanted. Luke is quick to point out that Peter and the others were astonished at the miracle that had taken place. Even if impulsive people are bold, they can still at times become paralyzed by fear. After all, fear was the original emotion expressed in the garden of Eden. Remember Adam's words, "I was afraid, because I was naked; and I hid myself" (Genesis 3:10). We all have things we're afraid of, including the future and the unknown. We may be afraid of failure or rejection. Who knows what combination of these or other fears may have come to rest in Peter's mind?

But Jesus compassionately urged Peter to give up his fear, then explained his new career and calling: "From now on, you will catch men" (Luke 5:10). As Warren Wiersbe points out in his book *Your Next Miracle*, Jesus didn't invent that phrase; it had been around for a long time. Greek philosophers and Jewish rabbis had used this image to describe "catching disciples by casting out the net of truth."[1] Jesus had a plan for Peter. He intended to use the skills, abilities, and persistence that had made Peter a good fisherman and refine the character flaws that were all too obvious at times. He would thus turn Peter into a man who had the stability of a rock in trusting his Savior and the tenacity of a fisherman in calling others to place their faith in the Lord. No wonder Peter became one of the most effective evangelists in the history of the church.

Impending Failure

One of the most significant encounters between this impetuous Galilean fisherman and his Master occurred during the Passover celebration in the upper room. Although John (13–16) included a great deal of detail regarding that poignant occasion, including the record of Jesus washing the disciples' feet, the identification of Judas as his betrayer, the promise of Christ's return to take them to a place he would be preparing, the provision of the Holy Spirit, and the power to serve the Lord in the face of persecution and adversity, only Luke recorded the pointed discussion between the Master and Peter. The interchange took place during a discussion about which of the disciples should be considered the greatest. Without question Peter must have been right in the middle of that discussion. After all, he had been recognized from the beginning as the leader of the group, even though in Matthew 20:20–21 the mother of James and John had demanded that her sons sit on Jesus' right and left sides.

Jesus wasted no time allowing this fruitless debate to continue. The Gentiles may look for authority and prominence, he pointed out at Luke 22:26, "But not so among you!" The words of Luke 22 are about as emphatic as the Greek language can get. On the contrary, he went on to explain, "He who is greatest among you, let him be as the younger, and he who governs as he who serves. . . . [and] I am among you as the One who serves" (vv. 26, 27). Frequently we become embroiled in the spirit of competition, seeking to boost our

stock at others' expense. Or we become overconfident in our service
to the Lord, perhaps based on previous successes. At such a time, we
are at great risk of spiritual danger, as was Peter.

Without hesitation the Lord turned to him and said, "Simon,
Simon! Indeed Satan has asked for you, that he may sift you as
wheat" (v. 31). It was a shocking warning to a man who was clearly
blinded by his own self-confidence. Ironically, the way Jesus phrased
the statement to Peter implies that both he and the other disciples
were at risk. Then the Lord continued, "I have prayed for you
[Peter], that your faith should not fail" (v. 32). What great assurance this statement should have given Peter. The Lord himself was
investing time interceding on his behalf, praying that his faith
would not be eclipsed by Satan's attack. Furthermore, Jesus expected his prayer to be answered: "When you have returned to Me,
strengthen your brethren," he instructed (v. 32).

Unfortunately, what Jesus had to say sailed right over Peter's
head, or perhaps went in one ear and out the other. "There's nothing
to worry about," Peter seemed to respond, "I'm ready to go with you
to prison or even to death." When things have been going well for
us, when God has been blessing, it's easy for us to become overconfident or to say, "I've handled those kinds of problems before. I can
handle them now." The Lord Jesus' next words carried a solemn note
of warning, "I tell you, Peter, the rooster shall not crow this day
before you will deny three times that you know Me" (v. 34).

Of course, Peter did then deny the Lord three times; and less
than a chapter later he remembered the word of the Lord, how he
had said to Peter, "Before the rooster crows you will deny me three
times." Then he responded with bitter tears (vv. 61, 62).

We might be tempted to think that Peter's career was over, that
the Lord would have no more use for him after such a denial. No,
Jesus recognized his weaknesses—his impulsiveness, his pride, even
his mixed-up priorities. And he had just the test for Peter, a test designed to overcome his traumatic failure and to prepare him for the
outstanding success he would soon experience on the day of Pentecost and beyond.

Peter's Final Exam

John 21 almost appears as a postscript to the Fourth Gospel, the gospel of the seven signs and the seamless robe. It follows on the heels of John's purpose statement, "These are written that you may believe that Jesus is the Christ, the Son of God, and that believing you may have life in His name" (v. 31). Ironically, much of this chapter revolves around Jesus and Peter. Peter and the others had been Jesus' disciples for over three years. They had witnessed the crucifixion; now they had seen the risen Lord. But they still had much to learn, especially Peter. Jesus knew that the best way to make sure that Peter and his colleagues remembered these lessons was to give them a test—sort of a final exam.

At first it appeared the disciples were going to flunk the test altogether. Peter, Thomas, Nathaniel, James, John, and two other disciples were together at the Sea of Galilee. Peter said, "I'm going fishing." Their response was, "We're right with you." They probably didn't have in mind a single excursion back to the lake or a pleasure trip to see if they had still their fishing skills. Peter had probably decided it was time to go back to the old career. They had followed Jesus for three years; he had promised to make them fishers of men. Then he died and had been resurrected. Peter needed to recall the lasting, life-changing impact of the Lord's call on his life. He needed, as he would put it later, to be stirred up by being reminded (2 Peter 1:13).

First, Jesus reminded him who was really in charge by testing Peter's patience. The men went fishing, spent the night on the lake of Galilee, and caught absolutely nothing. Now remember, these were professionals. Only once before had this ever happened to Peter—at least as far as we know—and that was in Luke 5. At daybreak Jesus stood on the shore, but the disciples didn't recognize him. "Catch anything, guys? Do you have any food?" he asked. "No," they replied. "Toss the net on the right side of the boat and you'll find some," he said. Do you see the parallel between what was happening here and what occurred earlier in Peter's life? In both instances the lesson was the same. Follow your own plan; use your own strength; and catch nothing. Follow the Lord's instructions, and you'll be overwhelmed with fish. When they were unable to draw the net into the boat because of the multitude of fish, John whispered to Peter, "It is the Lord!" (John 21:7).

When they arrived ashore, Peter experienced part two of his test—a test of his pride. John 21:9 records, "Then, as soon as they had come to land, they saw a fire of coals there, and fish laid on it, and bread." Two things must have burned themselves into Peter's mind as he stood there in the dim early morning light. First, there was a charcoal fire. The New Testament has only one other reference to a charcoal fire—the fire at which Peter was warming his hands when the servant girl accused him of being one of Jesus' companions, and he had vehemently denied her accusation that he had been one of his followers (Luke 22:55–57). Then to top off the humbling impact of the scene, fish were already laid out, along with bread. Where did Jesus get those fish? What a powerful reminder of something Jesus had said to them in the upper room the night before his crucifixion: "Without Me, you can do nothing" (John 15:5).

We don't like to be humbled any more than Peter did. Yet the Lord frequently uses the most humbling of circumstances to remind us of our past failures as well as to prepare us for our future successes. That's what Moses reminded the Israelites in Deuteronomy 8:16: "[He] fed you in the wilderness with manna . . . that He might humble you and that He might test you, to do you good in the end." Think of the sequence and how it parallels what happened with Peter: the Israelites had failed at Kadesh-Barnea; God humbled them, let them wander through the wilderness, tested them, and ultimately brought them triumphantly into the promised land. In the same fashion, God was humbling Peter in order to prepare him for future spiritual success.

Finally, Jesus tested Peter's priorities. Following the meal, the Lord three times asked Peter, "Do you love me more than these?" Peter's response was "Of course, Lord. . . . I feel so passionate about you." "Do you really?" Jesus asked. "If so, then become a shepherd of my sheep" (John 21:15–17; author's paraphrase). There's an obvious lesson for us in this interchange: the Lord desires our whole-hearted allegiance. His goal for each of us is that we love him most of all—with all our heart, soul, mind, and strength.

Peter immediately decided to approach his shepherding assignment the same way he did everything else—at full speed. "What about John? What should he do?" he asked (v. 21; author's paraphrase). Jesus replied, "Don't worry about John, Peter, you just concentrate on following me" (v. 22; author's paraphrase).

Purpose Fulfilled

From that point on, following Jesus is exactly what Peter did. He wasn't perfect, but the Lord began using Peter in a way almost beyond imagination, based on what had happened in his life before Jesus' death and resurrection. He preached boldly on the day of Pentecost, and three thousand people trusted Jesus as the Messiah. He and John healed a lame man, then courageously handled the questions of the high priest and his entourage. Peter's message to these Jewish leaders was clear-cut: "Nor is there salvation in any other, for there is no other name under heaven given among men by which we must be saved" (Acts 4:12). The leaders' response to this boldness, in light of the fact that Peter and John had no formal rabbinical training, was to realize "that they had been with Jesus"—the ultimate compliment (v. 13).

Later Peter and his colleagues were dramatically liberated from prison by an angel of the Lord and instructed to return to the temple and "speak to the people all the words of this life" (5:19, 20). When accused of filling Jerusalem with his doctrine, Peter and the others replied, "We ought to obey God rather than men" (5:29). Later God would use him to raise Tabitha, who was known as Dorcas, from the dead at Joppa (9:36–43), the same place where he received the divine message that God intended to include Gentiles in his plan of salvation. In Jerusalem a short time later, after Herod killed James, the brother of John, Peter was again locked in prison, only to be once again liberated by an angel from the Lord (12:7).

Near the end of his career, Peter wrote two epistles, in which he underscored many of the cardinal truths he had learned. For one thing the Lord's message about shepherding had been burned indelibly into his mind: "Shepherd the flock of God which is among you," he wrote, "serving as overseers, not by compulsion but willingly, not for dishonest gain but eagerly; nor as being lords over those entrusted to you, but being examples to the flock" (1 Peter 5:2, 3). Seeing himself as a fellow elder and shepherd, Peter called for service that was humble and eager and done for the right motive—the ultimate reward of God.

Finally, he wrapped up his last letter with words that seem to identify the key factor in his moving from risk taker to rock: "Keep growing in the grace and knowledge of our Lord Jesus Christ" (2 Peter 3:18; author paraphrase), he urged those to whom he wrote. Without question, Peter had learned the importance of desiring the authentic milk of the Word and growing thereby. The exuberant risk taker had trusted the Lord, answered his call, responded to the restoration test that followed his failure, and ultimately fulfilled the purpose God had for his life.

❧ Peter ❧

Take-Away Messages from the Past

1. No matter what our potential, we'll never amount to anything for God until we've trusted Christ and been transformed by his gospel.

2. The Lord has a mission for each of us, and it involves following him and fulfilling God's will.

3. We need to pay close attention to the Lord's warnings and be careful not to be overconfident.

4. Previous spiritual successes or victories do not exempt us from the danger of serious spiritual failures.

5. Even when we've failed miserably, the Lord can graciously extend to us an opportunity for restoration and even future service.

Choices for Today

1. If you haven't already done so, would you choose to turn from your sins to trust Jesus Christ as your Savior? After all, he died for you and rose again.

2. Would you choose to respond to his call to allow him to take control over every aspect of your life?

3. Is there one way today you would choose to temper your zest and enthusiasm with the wisdom that comes from spiritual growth?

4. Does your life contain any area of competitiveness and over-confidence that has gone too far and that you wish to ask God for help in balancing?

5. If you've failed miserably, would you choose to come back to a place of loving fellowship with the Lord?

Chapter Fifteen

Paul

Insane, Obsessive, or Genius?

What do accused terrorist Zacarias Moussaoui, former heavyweight boxer Mike Tyson, and Courtney Love (the widow of rock star Kurt Cobain) have in common? In addition to being controversial, all of them have undergone a psychiatric examination to determine whether or not they are sane.

In the mental health community today, the psychiatric exam is an extremely common tool. Far from being used only in criminal proceedings, psychiatric exams are required for some professionals, including airline pilots. A mental health clinic uses a mental evaluation to help the clinician determine whether or not a patient is sane; if a mental health issue exists, the exam can help the clinician decide how to treat it.

According to psychiatrist Dr. Mordecai Potash, assessing the psychiatric patient requires gathering identifying data; hearing the patient's chief complaint in his or her own words; developing a history of both the present illness and other psychiatric and medical factors; taking a family and medical history as well as a social history; giving a mental status exam dealing with mood, manic criteria, perceptual disturbances and thought processes; then developing a psychiatric report consisting of all data gathered from the interview and examination in a format that is informative to psychiatrists and allied mental health professionals.[1]

Many years ago Frank Minirth, while establishing his psychiatric practice and studying the life of the Apostle Paul, came up with the idea of applying modern psychiatric diagnostic criteria for a mental evaluation of the apostle. This innovative approach to considering the life of Paul is warranted by the fact that, on at least two occasions, the apostle's sanity was called into question. Paul himself raised the issue while writing to the Corinthians regarding the intensity of his commitment to Christ. Critics in Corinth had called into question the apostle's calling, sanity, and integrity. In response he pointed out, "We make it our aim, whether present or absent, to be well pleasing to Him" (2 Corinthians 5:9). Paul seemed to acknowledge that some of his critics would be quick to say, "Paul, you are crazy; you're insane." The apostle continued, "For if we are beside ourselves, it is for God; or if we are of sound mind it is for you" (5:13). Some of Paul's critics questioned his sanity, and the apostle acknowledged that the level of his commitment to God might open him to that question. The word he used, which is translated "to be beside oneself," is a term that "indicates mental imbalance."[2] Though Paul affirmed his sanity, he recognized that not everyone agreed.

Accused of Insanity

Later in his ministry, while Paul stood trial before Porcius Festus, the Roman procurator of Judea, and Herod Agrippa II, Festus interrupted the apostle's defense with the words "Paul, you are beside yourself. Much learning is driving you mad!" (Acts 26:24). The term translated "driving you mad" is a word that, according to *The New Linguistic and Exegetical Key to the Greek New Testament,* means to "be out of one's mind, to be insane. Those people are called crazy whose words or actions fly in the face of common sense, whose reasoning or conduct is not understood, who do not observe propriety and decorum."[3] We may at times casually label someone "crazy" or not; this definition can help us understand where such descriptions may actually apply.

Certainly, the Apostle Paul is one of the more intriguing characters of Scripture. Virtually all Bible scholars agree that he towers over the landscape of the New Testament: he is the author of thirteen of the twenty-seven New Testament books; he plays a central role in the history of the development of the early church as recorded in Luke's Acts; and his letters run the gamut from sophisticated theology (Romans) and philosophy (Colossians) to personal instruction and encouragement (Philemon, 2 Timothy).

So why evaluate this first-century apostle through the lens of modern psychiatry? Perhaps the most obvious reason is the fact that his contemporaries called his sanity into question. And although it isn't possible to bring him back to a psychiatrist's office for a mental evaluation, it is possible to take the information about Paul's life, including his own observations and those recorded by his companion and colleague Luke (a first-century physician), and come up with enough data to conduct a mental evaluation of the apostle. In doing so we believe we can achieve two important purposes. First, we can take a fresh look at the life of this unique individual and answer some questions that linger in the minds of many even today. Was Paul insane? Did he have an obsessive-compulsive disorder? Or was he a genius, a man of strong faith and extraordinary commitment to the cause to which he gave his life? Second, we can develop some points regarding his mental health that may apply to our lives and can help us make appropriate choices for living today.

A Remarkable Life

Although the mental evaluation itself will develop the apostle's history in more detail, we can note four major movements in his life: his early years in a Pharisaic home and under the influence of the great Jewish teacher, Gamaliel; his career as a Pharisee and intensely passionate opponent of the newly founded Christian faith; his conversion to Christ on the road to Damascus and subsequent commitment to preaching the gospel; and his career as a missionary, church planter, and writer of many New Testament epistles.

Paul's early life was unremarkable: he seems to have grown up in a very religious and perhaps strict home. He came from a proud ancestry, and his family claimed to be one of some prominence. When he was probably in his thirties, a remarkable event occurred as he traveled from Jerusalem to Damascus. After this event Paul changed the course of his life and became extremely zealous on behalf of the Christian faith, which he had previously persecuted. His remaining years were extremely productive as he wrote much of the New Testament. However, these years would also prove very turbulent. Paul suffered from many extreme situational problems, such as rejection by his own people, imprisonment, stoning, and beating. He made numerous difficult journeys around the Mediterranean Sea and became the first major missionary of the new Christian church. Eventually he would give his life as a martyr to the cause of Christ.

A careful study of the evidence about Paul demonstrates that enemies hounded him from the time of his conversion to Christ until his death. Some critics believe Paul was simply an obsessive-compulsive perfectionistic fanatic. Some have actually charged that he experienced a simple hallucination on the road to Damascus that left him mentally unbalanced. Others consider him one of the most brilliant and balanced individuals the world has ever known.

Let's examine the Apostle Paul using a formal mental evaluation, the same kind of psychiatric evaluation used in a modern mental health clinic. A typical mental evaluation includes the presenting picture, the history of the current issues under discussion, the past history, a mental exam, a dynamic formulation, and a diagnostic impression with recommendations.

The Presenting Picture

The presenting picture consists of one sentence summarizing the whole evaluation. It usually gives age, race, sex, residence, and chief complaint. The Apostle Paul was a middle-aged Jewish male from the city of Tarsus with a highly unusual story and set of life experiences that left him open to allegations of mental and emotional instability.

Was the apostle insane, as Festus charged? Did he have an obsessive-compulsive disorder? Or was he a genius? Was he a man of clear understanding and deep conviction, whose life and writings can be noted for spiritual direction even in the twenty-first century?

History of Present Problems

Had they had the luxury of psychiatric evaluations, numerous people with whom Paul came in contact might have requested that he be given a psychiatric exam. One of those would have been Festus, who believed Paul's diligent studies (perhaps both as a Pharisee and then as a follower of Christ) had led him to the brink of insanity and beyond (Acts 26:24). In addition, his chief critics in Corinth, who spent a great deal of time criticizing virtually everything about the apostle, would have insisted on a mental evaluation had such been available. Those Pharisaic colleagues with whom Paul had worked to undermine the Christian faith and imprison its proponents (Acts 9:1–2) must have thought that he had some kind of a mental breakdown that caused the radical shift in direction his life took after his experience on the road to Damascus.

Luke records the details of the incident on the road to Damascus in Acts 9:1–9. Breathing threats and murder against the disciples of the Lord, Paul (then known as Saul of Tarsus) requested letters from the high priest authorizing him to harass any followers of "the Way" (the term used for early Christians).

En route to Damascus, a light from heaven suddenly flashed, brighter than the sun at noon. Falling to the ground, Paul heard a voice, which he later acknowledged to be speaking in his native Hebrew (or Aramaic) tongue, "Saul, Saul, why are you persecuting me?" When he asked, "Who are you Lord?" Luke records the reply.

"I am Jesus whom you are persecuting. It is hard for you to kick against the goads." Trembling and astonished, Saul asked, "Lord, what do you want me to do?" To which the Lord replied, "Arise and go into the city and you will be told what you must do."

None of those traveling with the apostle saw anyone; all they heard was a voice.

Arising from the ground, Saul found himself blinded and had to be led by his companions to Damascus. There he became connected with a believer named Ananias, who was told by the Lord, "He is a chosen vessel of mine to bear my name before Gentiles, kings, and the children of Israel. For I will show him how many things he must suffer for my name's sake" (9:15–16).

From this point on, the apostle's life shifted to an exact opposite of what it had been. He would later claim to have seen and heard Jesus in person (22:6–10; 1 Corinthians 15:8).

Here we find that the apostle Paul had an unusual experience in which he both saw and heard things. This event changed the course of his life. He claims to have both heard and seen Jesus, who gave him a special mission for life.

Indeed, Paul's life did change after this experience. It left him with a deep and lifelong conviction. It was as though the strange light that came from the face of the glorified Christ had pierced his mind and soul. After that event, the apostle became as fervent for the church as he had before opposed it.

Out of that experience, Paul developed a single purpose in life, one that focused on living for Christ above all (Philippians 1:21) and that prompted him to refuse to be mastered by anything (1 Corinthians 6:12). Such a disciplined life almost seems impossible. For example, the apostle refused to do anything that would not profit and edify others and bring glory to God (10:23–33).

Even when facing the most stressful of circumstances, Paul persevered in his commitment to Christ: "But in all things we commend ourselves as ministers of God: in much patience, in tribulations, in needs, in distresses, in strifes, in imprisonments, in tumults, in labors, in sleeplessness, in fastings, by purity, by knowledge, by long-suffering, by kindness, by the Holy Spirit, by sincere love," he wrote in 2 Corinthians 6:4–6; and "As sorrowful yet always rejoicing; as poor, yet making many rich; as having nothing, and yet possessing all things" (v. 10).

Later the apostle told the Corinthians that, though his sanity was questioned, he had labored intensely; been imprisoned frequently;

been beaten often, including five instances where he received the maximum penalty of thirty-nine lashes; three times beaten with rods; once stoned; three times shipwrecked; and once spent a night and a day in the ocean before being rescued (11:23–25).

Without question the encounter with the penetrating light on the Damascus road left the Apostle Paul with a burning zeal to deliver a message from the Lord. That message provided good news to the Gentiles; it announced a new entity (the church); it unfolded a remarkable doctrine (grace); and it explained how to live the Christian life (by faith).

We should mention that the apostle had no previous experiences like the one described on the Damascus road.

As Dr. Minirth reviewed the apostle's problem, he could not help thinking, *Strange stories indeed. A very unusual man.* He has often identified people with similar stories as psychotic. Thus, he asked himself: Was the Apostle Paul insane, obsessive, a genius— or is there still another explanation?

Perhaps the apostle's past history and the formal mental evaluation will help.

Past History

Paul's life story was unusual, even from the start. A summary can be found in Philippians 3:5–6: "Circumcised the eighth day, of the stock of Israel, of the tribe of Benjamin, a Hebrew of Hebrews; concerning the law, a Pharisee; concerning zeal, persecuting the church; concerning the righteousness which is in the law, blameless."

Paul grew up in Tarsus, a city located in Cilicia, or present-day Turkey. He was of pure Jewish descent. As a child he was given the name of the first king of Israel (Saul) and was descended from King Saul's tribe, the tribe of Benjamin. The apostle inherited the rights of Roman citizenship. The date of Paul's birth is not known, but tradition gives it as the second year after Christ's birth. It seems that Paul grew up in a very strict Jewish home. It is safe to assume that he incorporated that strictness into his own conscience and that his very intense nature resulted in his becoming a leader against what he felt was a new heresy.

It seems he had reason to be proud and obsessive-compulsive (perfectionistic) in his personality traits. Many details that a psychiatrist usually obtains are missing, so we must draw insights by inference. Some of the interesting details that we can infer are as follows.

By Paul's own admission, Tarsus was "no mean city" (Acts 21: 39). It was a thriving emporium of trade and a focus of intellectual and religious activity. The mighty Tarsus Mountains lay to the north, and through the center of the city ran the Cydnus River. Tarsus had a thriving maritime trade, a university supported by the Roman Empire, and a high state of civic consciousness, thanks to which roads, bridges, arcades, and aqueducts were built. Nearby was the famous Cilician pass, a major trade route. Although Paul was born in Tarsus, he was not brought up there. According to accounts in Acts 22 and 26, the apostle was raised in the city of Jerusalem.

We are given very little direct information about Paul's parents. His father may have had a position of considerable importance and was undoubtedly a Roman citizen, since Paul exercised his own right to claim citizenship in the empire. Perhaps the apostle's father was given to sternness, because Paul described himself in his early years as "concerning the righteousness which is in the law, blameless" (Philippians 3:6). Paul wrote, "And you, fathers, do not provoke your children to wrath" (Ephesians 6:4). This latter statement would make one wonder if perhaps his father had been very stern.

No history is given about Paul's mother. Perhaps she died when he was young. In one of Paul's letters, he referred to the mother of Rufus as being his own mother, perhaps implying that he adopted her as a surrogate mother. In conclusion, although we know very little of the apostle's parents, we do know that Paul grew up as a very religious young man.

We know that Paul was of pure Hebrew stock. His genealogy was pure on both sides. In all likelihood, the Hebrew tongue was the ordinary language of the household. As we noted, Luke recorded of Paul's encounter with Jesus on the Damascus road that the Lord spoke to Paul in Hebrew (Acts 26:14). The apostle must have taken great pride in the fact that he belonged to God's chosen race, the Hebrews—the race to whom the covenants and the Law had been given; the people with ancestors such as Abraham, Isaac, Jacob, Moses, Elijah, Samuel, David, and Daniel. It was a noble ancestry indeed. Perhaps he bore the name of Israel's first king, Saul, with some mixture of feelings. He may have been determined to bear that name and not fail God, as his namesake had.

According to modern psychotherapy, Paul would have many internal injunctions and a firm life-script. His life-script was centered around doing right and being responsible, or to put it in his own words, "concerning the righteousness which is in the law, blameless" (Philippians 3:6).

Paul's mentor had been the famous Hebrew rabbi, Gamaliel (Acts 22:3). Paul must have had an extremely keen mind. He must have been a very disciplined individual to have been permitted to sit at the feet of a teacher held in such high regard.

As a youth, Paul learned the trade of tent making. It was customary that each Jewish boy should learn a trade, and Paul was no exception. He learned a trade that, although he did not realize it at the time, would prove to be an extremely helpful occupation throughout his ministry career.

Following his deeply religious childhood, Paul continued as a young adult to follow strict Hebrew beliefs. Before long he began persecuting what he felt was a new heresy, Christianity. In Acts 8 we find him in agreement with and actually participating indirectly in the stoning of Stephen. The death of this courageous, godly man must have left a deep impression on Paul.

In Acts 9 we find the story of Paul's conversion experience. After the encounter with Jesus on the Damascus road, Paul entered Damascus and met a godly man named Ananias, who provided the new believer with early mentoring in the faith.

Paul then spent three years in the Arabian Desert in seclusion (Galatians 1:17). Afterward, he returned to Damascus for three years of preaching (1:17b–18). In the face of mounting pressure from the Jews, he returned to Jerusalem, hoping to visit with Peter (1:18). However, as they had in Damascus, the Jews rose up against Paul, so he left Jerusalem for Tarsus (Acts 9:29–30). He spent several years there, then joined Barnabas in ministry in Antioch (11: 25–26). A large number of people had recently come to trust Christ there, and they needed Paul's assistance. When persecution broke out in Jerusalem, Barnabas and Paul were sent with relief to aid believers there (11:29–30). After fulfilling their mission to Jerusalem, the two returned to Antioch (12:25).

Over the years the apostle would undertake three missionary journeys. The first included stops at Cyprus, Salamis, Perga, Antioch of Pisidia, Iconium, Lystra, and Derbe (Acts 13–14). On the second missionary journey, Paul visited Macedonia, Philippi, Thessalonica, Berea, Athens, and Corinth (Acts 16–18). His third missionary journey included visits to Ephesus, Troas of Macedonia, and Miletus (Acts 19–20). Eventually, Paul was arrested in Jerusalem and ultimately was sent to Rome for trial (Acts 21–28). After his first Roman imprisonment, Paul continued his ministry and labors. He was eventually imprisoned again, although he was charged with nothing except preaching Christ. We have no record of the final stages of his trial. According to tradition, Paul was subsequently imprisoned, then martyred by decapitation.

His past history can be organized into nine or ten major areas. An outline of the typical notes from a psychiatric exam of the Apostle Paul follows. Some of the text will repeat earlier information noted; this information is repeated in a form common to the formal mental evaluation.

Early Development

Paul was born in Tarsus but brought up in Jerusalem. His early history seems rather unremarkable, with the exception that it seemed that he grew up in an extremely strict and highly religious environment.

History of Father

Very little is said about Paul's father. He may have been very stern. Because Paul was born a Roman citizen (Acts 22:28), his father must have been a Roman citizen before him. The apostle on more than one occasion appealed to his rights as a Roman citizen (16:37; 22:25; 25:11). Because it was customary for Jewish fathers to pass along both biblical values (Deuteronomy 6:4–5) and a trade, Paul apparently "Learned to make cilicium, a goat's hair cloth used for tents, sails and cloaks. In later years, as Paul traveled from church to church, he used his trade as a livelihood and became well known as a tent maker."[4]

History of Mother

No history is given about Paul's mother. By inference, we may wonder how much or how long she was present in Paul's life.

Siblings

Little history is given regarding Paul's siblings. There is one reference to a sister. In Acts 23:16 Luke refers to "Paul's sister's son," stating Paul's nephew heard of a planned ambush and warned Paul of it.

Schooling

The apostle was an extremely well-educated man. As a youth, he became a student of Gamaliel, a distinguished Jewish teacher of the Pharisaic school of Hillel, the strictest branch of Pharisaism. Considering Paul's education and early prominence, we might assume that he came from a family of means and social stature. We also know that his education was very religiously oriented. Note that although Paul was well educated, he apparently was not an articulate or persuasive speaker (2 Corinthians 10:10). In addition to his Jewish education under Gamaliel, the apostle appears to have had knowledge of the well-known Greek poets of the day (Acts 17:28) and of Gnostic religious thought (Colossians 2:8).

Marriages

None recorded, although Pharisees were typically married. Perhaps he was a widower.

Children

None. There is one brief reference to a sister and a nephew (Acts 23:16).

Occupation

The apostle practiced the trade of tent making, which he had learned as a youth. He later became extremely active in pursuing his Jewish faith and persecuting the newly established Christian church. After his conversion, he became a missionary for the Christian faith. He also continued his tent-making trade while carrying out missionary service in order to provide his own support.

Health

The apostle had some sort of physical illness that caused him a great deal of trouble. He referred to it as his "thorn in the flesh" (2 Corinthians 12:7) but gave no details. Many biblical scholars have suggested that it was an eye disease (see Galatians 4:15; 6:11).

Past Psychiatric History

Paul makes only one reference to typical types of problems that everyone suffers from, such as "conflicts on the outside, fears within" (2 Corinthians 7:5 NIV). In similar fashion he referred to himself as "sorrowful, yet always rejoicing" (6:10). "We are hard-pressed on every side, yet not crushed; we are perplexed, but not in despair; persecuted, but not forsaken; struck down, but not destroyed" (4:8, 9).

He never considered his conversion experience, during which he claimed to have seen the Lord, to be a hallucination. Rather, he related it to the supernatural purpose of God (Galatians 1:15). He insisted that he had, in fact, seen the Lord (1 Corinthians 9:1; 15:8).

Mental Exam

The typical mental exam contains seven categories: general appearance; intellectual functions; communication; thought, form, and content; mood; insight; and judgment. The following is how they might be recorded for the Apostle Paul.

General Appearance

We find some hints of Paul's general appearance in his letters to the Corinthians. However, much of our impression comes by inference and tradition. In 1 Corinthians 2:3 the apostle notes: "And I was with you in weakness, in fear, and in much trembling." Then in 2 Corinthians 10:10 he observes: "'For his letters,' they say, 'are weighty and powerful, but his bodily presence is weak, and his speech contemptible.'"

From these references we can see that the apostle was quite open in admitting to anxiety and weakness, that his appearance was apparently unimpressive, and that he was not an eloquent speaker or orator. According to tradition, Paul was short (the name *Paul* means "little") with thin hair, crooked legs, thick eyebrows, and a bent nose; yet he was full of grace. That final observation seems consistent with 2 Corinthians 10:1 (NIV), where Paul admitted, "I . . . am 'timid' when face to face with you, but 'bold' when away!" The apostle was very gracious in general, but he could be quite bold if he felt it necessary, both in his correspondence and in person. For example, he demonstrated significant boldness when he felt constrained to confront the Apostle Peter over the issue of not fellowshipping with Gentile Christians (Galatians 2:11).

Paul was a man of great zeal, untiring industry, singleness of purpose, patience in suffering, and tremendous courage. He faced unbelievable hardships against overwhelming odds. We also see in him a fearless independence, evidenced by his willingness to challenge the most influential church leader, Peter. He could confront whole churches, as he did in his Galatian and Corinthian letters. Yet his letters to Philemon and the Philippians show great sensitivity.

The cumulative evidence of his letters presents him as a man who sought to avoid any appearance of evil (2 Corinthians 1:12) and who labored that he might not be chargeable (under obligation) to any person (2 Thessalonians 3:8). He was quick to communicate appropriate affirmation and praise, as we see in the introductions to his epistles (1 Corinthians 1:1, 2; Ephesians 1:1; 1 Timothy 1:1, 2). He was marked by authentic love, as is evidenced by the way he gave of himself to the many churches that he helped establish (2 Corinthians 12:15). He was concerned over the sins of others; yet he was very personal, often mentioning fellow believers by name (Romans 16: 1–17). His words to Timothy in his final letter reflect his desire for closeness with his brothers and sisters in Christ (2 Timothy 4:9–13).

In summary, we find a man who, although unimpressive in outward appearance, demonstrated great mental and spiritual abilities, yet manifesting those abilities in a balanced manner.

Intellectual Functions

Paul seemed to function at a very high, even superior, intellectual level. From all available evidence, he was well oriented (aware of himself and his surroundings), alert, and not confused. He had no problems with memory. He had a high level of educational attainment, as reflected in his writings.

Communication

Paul's communication was logical, rational, and coherent. Some of his communication was obviously very deep, but in no sense could it be considered irrational.

Thought, Form, and Content

Although Paul had one major purpose in life—to advance the church of Christ—the content of his writing was extensive. He discussed such topics as natural revelation, the universality of sin, justification, faith, original sin, union with Christ, the status of Israel as a nation, spiritual gifts, respect for government, the judgment seat of Christ, the Holy Spirit, love, sexuality, the resurrection, the church, the preeminence of Christ, the events of the last days, the role of women in the church, qualifications for elders and deacons, the care of widows, the use of money, and a variety of other topics. He showed no history of obsessions or phobias, and his language was clear and coherent.

Mood

Neither the apostle's record in Acts nor his epistles give any history of clinical depression or neurotic anxiety. Paul was very open in talking about perfectly understandable fears, anxiety, and conflicts, given the pressures he faced (2 Corinthians 4:8–10).

Insight

Paul gave every indication of having very good insight and self-understanding, particularly concerning his weaknesses (Romans 7:7–25).

Judgment

Paul evidenced good judgment. He worked tirelessly, giving his life to what he believed in (2 Timothy 4:7). His life was marked by generosity toward others. His letters indicate balance in decision making (Romans 1:11–13). His relationships with people show him to be a man of help, love, and discernment (Philemon 10–22).

Dynamic Formulation

The dynamic formulation is a one-paragraph summary that ties together all the major factors that explain a person's mental health or lack thereof. It usually includes six factors: genetics, early environmental factors, basic personality, basic defenses, religious history, and precipitating stress. These factors do not negate one another; rather, they must be integrated. We can see God behind each factor in Paul's life.

Paul apparently came from a good genetic background, or as we might express it, from healthy stock. His early environment was unremarkable with the exception of his stern, Pharisaic religious environment. He likely grew up with a number of obsessive-compulsive traits including a strong sense of duty and dedication and a strict conscience. However, he evidenced significant balance in his basic personality. His major defenses were a generally healthy tolerance, forgiveness, security, and faith. Paul probably became a Christian in his thirties; and although he faced many stresses during subsequent years, he maintained good mental and emotional health.

In conclusion, he was not insane, nor did he have an obsessive-compulsive personality disorder. Rather, his great mental and spiritual abilities, as previously noted, probably earn him the designation genius; he was extremely godly; and he had a very healthy personality. He was a very determined, focused individual who never lost sight of his mission. He had "fought the good fight" and "kept the faith" (2 Timothy 4:7).

Diagnostic Impression

After weighing all the factors as a psychiatrist, Dr. Minirth's conclusion is that the Apostle Paul was an extremely mentally healthy individual. His history was compatible with what we would expect of a balanced and dependable individual. He was other-centered rather than self-centered. He had an effective support system consisting of people around him, and he took pains to communicate with them, as is evidenced by the many people to whom he made reference by name in his letters. He was confident in facing his environmental stressors. He shared balanced emotional expression and control.

In short, all the traits we can observe from Paul's life indicate a very healthy individual. His mental health was evidenced by the lack of symptoms that indicate pathology. For example, there was no history of clinical depression or of intense anxiety. There was no history of hallucinations or delusions. His conversion encounter, as verified by Scripture, should be considered a legitimate experience. An individual who had delusional experiences would most likely have symptoms of schizophrenia, such as an inability to develop close relationships, a history of incoherent and illogical conversation, and loose associations. Paul had no such history. Rather, he maintained close relationships, and his writing was logical and coherent. He did not seem paranoid. Neither did the apostle fit the other common types of psychosis, such as manic-depressive disorder with increased speech, increased motor activity, and euphoria. Nor did he fit any paranoid psychotic disorder.

No doubt Paul had some obsessive-compulsive personality traits, especially prior to his conversion (see Philippians 3:4–6). However, he certainly did not have an obsessive-compulsive personality disorder, and he reflected a significant degree of balance after his conversion.

Thus, the apostle could not have been insane. He did not have a personality disorder. He showed evidence of being a genius, and he exhibited a very keen mind. He was also able to apply his abilities to effect a major change in the future of humankind. Dr. Minirth believes that Paul's genius came about because of God's work in his life. It seems God chose this man for the greatest spiritual purpose during and since New Testament times, other than Jesus Christ himself.

The Apostle Paul was not perfect. He was very open in describing his own anxieties, conflicts, and weaknesses. He wrestled with "all manner of evil desire" (Romans 7:8), a significant area of temptation for those with obsessive-compulsive traits. He also struggled with pride (2 Corinthians 12:7). In fact, God, who knows everything, found it necessary to give Paul a thorn in the flesh to help suppress his prideful tendencies. Paul knew this and kept asking to have it removed (just like us, he would have preferred life to be easier!). Further, Paul knew what it was like to experience conflict with a good friend (Barnabas) and have both feel they were right (Acts 15:36–39). Yet all in all, Paul was a healthy, mature, godly man.

Recommendations

Recommendations are customary in psychiatric evaluations. In this case Dr. Minirth's recommendations are not for the Apostle Paul but rather for the readers. All of us need to follow Paul's advice, identify with him, and learn from him. Not only can we identify with things in the apostle's life, but we should also try to take his advice. Take Romans 1:16, which seems to reflect Paul's life mission: "For I am not ashamed of the gospel of Christ, for it is the power of God to salvation for everyone who believes, for the Jew first and also for the Greek."

Develop a Purpose in Life

Frank Minirth recalls how he learned not to be ashamed of the gospel as a young college student studying the Bible with one of his peers. Frank remembers that his voice trembled as he told his friend of Christ. Many thoughts ran through Frank's mind as to what the friend would think of him. A few years later, when Frank finished medical school, he received a letter from this friend, telling Frank that he now trusted Christ and that he too had entered medical school. Frank has since had the privilege of working with him and helping him grow further in the Lord.

From this incident in his life comes the first of our recommendations: to develop a purpose or mission in life, one that centers around knowing Christ personally and making him known to others. For Paul nothing was more important than cultivating an intimate, growing relationship with Jesus Christ. As he explained it, "Yet indeed I also count all things less for the excellence of the knowledge of Christ Jesus my Lord, for whom I have suffered the loss of all things, and count them as rubbish that I may gain Christ and be found in Him, not having my own righteousness which is from the law, but that which is through faith in Christ, the righteousness which is from God by faith; that I may know Him and the power of His resurrection and the fellowship of His sufferings, being conformed to His death" (Philippians 3:8–10).

From Paul's commitment to know Christ and make him known, we can develop three important implications. First, like Paul, we must have a personal encounter with Christ. We may not have the kind of dramatic encounter he experienced on the road to Damascus, yet each of us must acknowledge our sin and need of a savior and trust the Lord Jesus who died for us and rose again. If you have never done so, now would be an ideal time. Simply take a moment and bow before the Lord and admit, "Lord Jesus, I am a sinner. I believe you died for me and rose again, and I trust you to save me."

For those of us who have trusted the Lord, cultivating that intimate, personal knowledge of him comes through spending time daily in his Word. Although he is not present with us physically today, we can gain that close relationship reflected in Paul's statement in Philippians 3 by carving out a time to read God's Word and get to know him and by sharing our thoughts and concerns with him in prayer.

A natural outgrowth of this is the desire to make Christ known to others. All three authors have had the privilege of sharing Christ in ministry, including on radio, in public-speaking ministry, and most important of all, in one-on-one encounters. There is no greater privilege and responsibility than representing the Savior who loved us and gave himself for us.

Deal with Your Thorn in the Flesh

Throughout his life the apostle suffered adversity; yet nothing seemed to affect him quite like the thorn in the flesh, a significant physical adversity that Scripture never identified but for which Paul "pleaded with the Lord three times" for relief (2 Corinthians 12:8). Frank Minirth considered diabetes mellitus, with which he was diagnosed at age twelve, as his thorn in the flesh; and his experience paralleled that of Paul, who found God's grace sufficient and divine strength made perfect in human weakness (12:9). Whatever your area of suffering, remember to ask God to give you the grace to endure.

Cultivate an Appreciation of the Grace of God

Although each of the three authors, like Paul, was raised in a strict home, we have had the privilege of coming to a greater understanding of the grace of God over the years. In his letter to the Galatians, Paul particularly emphasized God's grace and the liberty it provided. In 1 Corinthians 15:10 he mentions God's grace three times: first, as the means by which God made the apostle who he was; second, as the key to security ("His grace toward me was not in vain"); and finally, as the ultimate source of energy and strength for serving God.

One verse that has become deeply ingrained into each of the authors' minds is Paul's confession of how he lived: "I have been crucified with Christ; it is no longer I who live, but Christ lives in me; and the life which I now live in the flesh I live by faith in the Son of God, who loved me and gave Himself for me" (Galatians 2:20).

Make Memorizing and Meditating on Scripture a Priority

Near the end of his life, Paul wrote to Timothy, the young man he mentored. One of his main encouragements was "Be diligent to present yourself approved to God, a worker who does not need to be ashamed, rightly dividing the word of truth" (2 Timothy 2:15). Using language that came from his trade as a tent maker, the apostle urged his protégé to be sure to "cut" the word accurately, just as a tent maker would measure carefully and cut the cloth from which he made his product accurately. Paul went on to underscore the value of God's inspired Word for showing us what to believe, for pointing out when we are engaged in wrongdoing, for getting us on the right track, and for instructing us in right living. In short, Paul believed that Scripture was the ultimate tool for equipping God's people for every good work (3:16–17). For each of us, memorization of Scripture (through programs such as Navigator's, Bible Memory Association, CBM Ministry, and others) has provided the resource for meditation, spiritual strength, insight, and growth.

Follow Paul's Formula for Dealing with Worry

Those of us who have some obsessive traits, as Paul did, may have a tendency to worry. Perhaps he was sharing from his own experience when he wrote to the Philippians (4:6), "Be anxious for nothing, but in everything by prayer and supplication, with thanksgiving, let your requests be made known to God." Whenever we authors have faced times of anxiety, this verse, and the following promise of the "peace of God which surpasses all understanding" (v. 7) has provided significant encouragement and strength. So remember: when you find yourself caught up in worry, use your worries as a signal to turn to the Lord in prayer.

Look for Opportunities to Mentor Others

For Paul the process of discipling, as practiced by the Lord Jesus, was to be an ongoing priority in the lives of believers in his day and in ours. As he wrote to Timothy to encourage him to be strong in the grace of Christ, he instructed, "And the things that you have heard from me among many witnesses, commit these to faithful men who will be able to teach others also" (2 Timothy 2:2). Earlier Paul had identified Timothy as his "true son in the faith" (1 Timothy 1:2); and Paul had clearly invested a great deal of his time instructing Timothy and modeling principles of Christian living, growth, and service. Now the apostle was about to depart this earth, and he felt it a vital necessity to urge Timothy to carry on the discipling or mentoring process, selecting and training trustworthy individuals who would be able to instruct others as Timothy instructed them.

Each of us authors has had the privilege of having mentors who influenced our lives, and likewise each of us has had the joy of investing in the lives of others in discipling relationships. After all, if Jesus' last word of instruction before ascending from this earth was "Go . . . and make disciples" (Matthew 28:19), then that needs to be the priority for us, as it was for Paul.

Live Each Day in Light of the Judgment Seat of Christ

In 2 Corinthians 5:9 Paul underscored his aim, "Whether present or absent, to be well pleasing to Him." Then he explained his motivation. Each of us, he noted, must appear before the judgment seat of Christ to have our works evaluated, whether good or bad (v. 10). As he had explained to the Corinthians earlier, every believer's work will be tested as by fire to determine whether it is of enduring worth (1 Corinthians 3:12–15). Some works, done for the wrong motive or in the wrong manner, will be judged as worthless, whereas others, done for the glory of God and in his power, will be rewarded. Like Paul, we authors have cultivated great respect for our Savior and strive to please him in every thought, word, and deed. We haven't arrived yet, but knowing that someone like Paul set such an incredible example motivates us to fight the good fight, run the race, and keep the faith (2 Timothy 4:7).

🍃 Paul 🍃

Take-Away Messages from the Past

1. The Apostle Paul was a genius, according to this evaluation. He produced in ways never dared before; he had extraordinary intellect, ingenuity, and production; he was not obsessive or insane. God enabled Paul to be the way he was.

2. Much can be learned from seeing the totality of a person's life and current functionality. Not only can we learn from Paul, but we can also apply his genius to our lives.

3. Paul was a man of great vision; his strong desire was to preach Christ where others had not been to share the good news of forgiveness and grace (Romans 15:20).

4. Paul was a man of significant balance. For example, on the core message of the gospel, he condemned those who differed (Galatians 1:8). Upon matters of individual conscience, he demonstrated greater flexibility (1 Corinthians 8).

5. Paul was incredibly adaptable, as he explained to the Corinthians. To the Jews he operated as a Jew (though not in bondage to the Law); to Gentiles, to the weak, and to the strong, he became "all things to all men" that he might reach them for Christ (1 Corinthians 9:19–23).

Choices for Today

1. What innate trait do you have that God might develop? Would you be willing to ask him to do so? Would you even ask if he might give you extraordinary gifts and abilities to be used in his service?

2. What insights have you gained as you reviewed Paul's life? Have you made any new choices?

3. What vision, what dream, have you cultivated that you believe God wants you to pursue? Is it a dream that involves significant service to Christ?

4. Ask yourself: Do those who know me best see me as a balanced individual? Are my convictions strong on those nonnegotiables? Am I flexible in matters that are not spelled out in Scripture?

5. Have I learned to be adaptable to individuals, to approach different people differently in order to reach them for Christ and to build them up in the faith? Perhaps I can learn from Paul's example in this area.

Conclusion

We have now reached the end of our journey through the lives of these biblical characters. Take a moment to consider whose life most closely affected you. Could you relate to the ordinariness of Gideon? Have you struggled with adversity and bitterness like Naomi or Job? Have people questioned your sanity as they did Paul's? Maybe, like Martha, you have been focused on performing; or like Elijah, you may seem somewhat perfectionistic. Like Moses or Peter, your life may have been marked with ups and downs.

Consider three important overriding things as you think back over the lives of the biblical individuals we have considered in *Just Like Us*.

We Can Relate to Them

If there is one lesson we have learned throughout our journey, it's that these were not superheroes. We haven't been studying the lives of Batman, Superman, or Wonder Woman. Though they accomplished many extraordinary feats, these biblical figures did not do so out of lives of perfection. Frequently they struggled; sometimes they failed—and failed miserably. In every instance we can relate to what they experienced. Like David, we've experienced victory but tasted defeat. Like Elijah, we sought perfection but haven't achieved it. Like John the Baptist, at times we've seemed out of step with those around us.

We Can Learn from Them

The point in *Just Like Us* is not simply to show how we can all connect with these biblical characters or even to show how their experiences parallel ours. Instead, as authors we wanted to present the many lessons all of us can learn from the lives of Solomon, Peter, Hezekiah, Naomi, and Jeremiah. Perhaps this would be a good time to sit down, take a piece of paper, and draw a line down the middle. On the left side, write the names of three or four of the characters in *Just Like Us* that seem to have the most impact on you. Then on the other side of the page, jot down two or three practical lessons you can remember from reading about the lives of each of them. Go back to the chapters for review, if you like. After all, the three key laws of learning are repetition, repetition, and . . . well, you can probably figure out the third. Go back and review these characters and allow God to reinforce the lessons you have learned from this book. And then pass them on to others.

We Can Use the Same Power They Experienced

Finally, and perhaps most important of all, is the lesson that these individuals—despite their sins, failures, and struggles—came in contact with the infinite power of a supernatural God—the God of Scripture, the God who sent his Son, Jesus Christ, to die on the cross to pay for our sins and rise again to provide us with the power for successful, healthy living. To some degree each of these individuals was able to tap into that power—by faith. Faith isn't some nebulous concept; it's simply exercising trust that goes beyond our own abilities. It is trusting Christ, who he is and what he did through the cross and his resurrection, for our salvation. In the same way, we learn to live day by day in dependence on him (see Paul's explanation of this in Colossians 2:6–7). And as we trust him to work in our lives, in the daily routine, as he did with ordinary people like Gideon, Caleb, and Martha, we'll see him accomplish extraordinary things, for his glory.

Notes

Preface

1. R. D. Ornstein, "Trauma and Posttraumatic Stress Disorder," in T. A. Stern and J. B. Herman, eds., *Psychiatry Update and Board Preparation* (New York: McGraw-Hill, 2000), 129.
2. B. Reddick and N. Cassem, "Treatment Decisions at the End of Life," in Stern and Herman, *Psychiatry Update and Board Preparation*, 515.
3. P. Smallwood, "Personality Disorders," in Stern and Herman, *Psychiatry Update and Board Preparation*, 189.
4. J. A. Lieberman III, "The Primary Care Physician's Role in Treating Mental Illness," *Drug Benefit Trends*, 2003, *15* (April, supp. B), 24.

Chapter One: Gideon

1. "Cheeks Anthem Assist" (2003). (http://www.nba.com/blazers/features/Cheeks_Anthem_Assist-73713-41.html)
2. "Urban Legends Reference Pages: Humor (Pizza Spy)" (1995). (http://www.snopes.com/humor/jokes/fbipizza.htm)
3. G. Edwards, "Sea of Fire," *Spin*, Sept. 2000, p. 111.
4. Campus and Education Jokes, "Ohio State Calculus Final Story" (n.d.). (http:www.absolutelyjokes.com/campus-and-educations/assignment/ohio-state-calculus-final-story.html)
5. J. Falwell, "The Wonderful Adventure of Bill Bright," *WorldNet-Daily*, July 26, 2003 (http.//www.worldnetdaily.com/news/article.as;?ARTICLE_ID=33768).

6. "William R. 'Bill' Bright, Founder of World's Largest Christian Ministry, Dies" (Sept. 18, 2003). (http://billbright.cci.org/public/index.htm)

Chapter Two: Job

1. "Col. Floyd J. Thompson, 69; Longest-Held POW: 9 Years in Vietnam" (North Sports Final Edition, obituary, New York Times News Service), *Chicago Tribune*, July 19, 2002, p. 8.
2. Certainly some suffering is due to sin (1 Corinthians 11:30), but not all.
3. M. Lucado, *In the Eye of the Storm* (Dallas: Word Publishing, 1991), 11.

Chapter Three: Moses

1. Paul D. Meier and Frank B. Minirth, *Introduction to Psychology and Counseling* (Grand Rapids, Mich.: Baker Book House, 1982), 184.
2. (http://www.geocities.com/ptypes/cyclothymicpd.html)
3. *Josephus, the Essential Works*, trans. and ed. by Paul Maier (Grand Rapids, Mich.: Kregel, 1988), 47–48.
4. Ibid., p. 48.
5. Review the contents of the following references: Abraham, Genesis 22:11; Moses, Exodus 3:4; Samuel, 1 Samuel 3:10; the residents of Jerusalem, Matthew 23:37; Martha, Luke 10:41; Peter, Luke 22:31; and Saul (Paul), Acts 9:4.

Chapter Four: Caleb

1. *Chariots of Fire* (Buena Vista, Touchstone, 1981).
2. J. Gilmore, *Ambushed at Sunset: Coping with Mature Adult Temptations* (San Antonio: LangMarc, 1997).
3. W. Wiersbe, "Your Senior Years Can Be Fruitful," *Moody Monthly*, Feb. 1974, p. 38.
4. "Confident Living" (radio broadcast), Oct. 23, 1999.

Chapter Five: Naomi

1. T. H. Holmes and R. H. Rahe, "Social Readjustment Rating Scale," *Journal of Psychosomatic Research*, 1967, 2, 213–218.
2. Pastor and Bible teacher Ray Stedman coined this phrase (see http://www.pbc.org/dp/stedman/adventure/0208.html).

Chapter Six: David

1. From "Othello," Act III, Scene iii, lines 173–175, in *The Complete Works of William Shakespeare* (Garden City, N.Y.: Country Life Press, 1936), 956.

Chapter Seven: Solomon

1. "The Mysterious Love Affair of Katherine Hepburn and Spencer Tracy" (July 30, 2003). (http://www.magisociety.com/hepburntracy.htm)
2. American Social Health Association, "STD Statistics" (retrieved Nov. 26, 1998). (http://www.ahsastd.org/stdfaqs/statistics.html)
3. K. Stabiner, "The Problem with Kids Today? Today's Parents, Some Say," *New York Times*, June 25, 2000, p. WH14.
4. (http://www.robertperkinson.com/alcoholism_statistics.htm)

Chapter Eight: Elijah

1. D. G. Benner, ed., *Christian Counseling and Psychotherapy* (Grand Rapids, Mich.: Baker Book House, 1987), 79.
2. Adapted from the perfectionism quiz found in D. Augsberger, *When Enough Is Enough* (Ventura, Calif.: Regal Books, 1984), 152.
3. The name was considered so holy that Israelites would not pronounce it.
4. J. Hampton Keathley, "Studies in the Life of Elijah" (1995). (http://www.bible.org/docs/ot/character/elijah/toc.html)

Chapter Nine: Hezekiah

1. A. W. Tozer, *The Pursuit of God* (Harrisburg, Pa.: Christian Publishers, 1948), 14.
2. M. Conklin, "Rage!" *Chicago Tribune*, July 28, 2000, p. 1.
3. J. B. Smith, *R. Mullins: An Arrow Pointing to Heaven* (Nashville: Broadman and Holman, 2000), 44–45.

Chapter Ten: Jeremiah

1. C. Pfeiffer, ed., *The Wycliffe Bible Commentary* (Chicago: Moody Press, 1962), 656.
2. Scholars still debate the authorship of Lamentations. Jewish tradition associates it with Jeremiah. Dr. R. K. Harrison notes, "In favor of Jeremiah as author are the obvious similarities in style and subject matter which both works exhibit. . . . While the authorship of the work must necessarily remain unknown, it seems highly improbable that anyone other than Jeremiah would have been moved to such depths of elegiac expression by the collapse of resistance in Jerusalem and still be in a position to record his feelings in such moving verse" ("Jeremiah and Lamentations," in D. J. Wiseman, gen. ed., *Tyndale Old Testament Commentaries*, Downers Grove, Ill.: Inter-Varsity Press, 1973, 198).
3. C. Dyer, Dallas Theological Seminary class notes, "Exilic and Post-Exilic Prophets," Bible 304, Mar. 1982.
4. H. E. Freeman, *An Introduction to the Old Testament Prophets* (Chicago: Moody Press, 1968), 246.

Chapter Eleven: Daniel

1. Holmes and Rahe (1967).

Chapter Twelve: John

1. B. Graham, "The Signs of His Coming," *Decision*, Nov. 1980, p. 2.
2. (www.wordskit.com/quotes)

3. J. White, "The Power of Integrity," *Discipleship Journal*, Mar.-
   Apr. 1998, n.p. (http://www.navpress.com/Magazines/DJ/
   ArticleDisplay.asp?mscsid=C03AG2AAD8658PJJ2TH5FSRF
   DGXF89JB&ID=104.02) James S. McDonnell began his business (McDonnell Aircraft Corp.) July 6, 1939; Donald W. Douglas began his (Douglas Aircraft Co.) July 22, 1920. The merger
   of the two companies was official on Apr. 28, 1967. James
   Smith McDonnell, then sixty-eight, was chairman of the board
   of directors and CEO of the new McDonnell Douglas Corp.
   Donald Douglas Sr., seventy-five, was honorary chairman of the
   merged corporation. The entire story is at http://www.boeing.
   com/history/.
4. C. Cutrer, "Soul Survivor," *Today's Christian Woman*, July-Aug.
   2003, p. 50.
5. *Addresses by Henry Drummond* (Chicago: Bible Institute Col-
   portage Association, 1898), 115.

Chapter Thirteen: Martha

1. Formally known as the DISC Profile and Dimensions of Behavior.
   (http://www.internalchange.com/disc_profile_store/mall/
   ProductPage1.asp?sourc) See also W. Marston, *Emotions of Normal
   People* (Minneapolis: Persona Press, 1979).
2. J. S. Chanen, "Try a Little Typecasting," *ABA Journal*, Nov.
   2000, 86(11), 68; I. B. Myers, *Gifts Offering: Understanding Personality Type* (Palo Alto, Calif.: Davies-Black, 1995).
3. R. Hatley, "Personality Types" (Apr. 2000). (http://home.
   pacbell.net/earnur/essays/personality-types.html)
4. G. Smalley and J. Trent, *The Two Sides of Love* (Pomona, Calif.:
   Focus on the Family, 1990).
5. M. Friedman and R. Rosenman, *Type A Behavior and Your Heart*
   (New York: Knopf, 1974).
6. D. Stack, *Martha to the Max* (Chicago: Moody Press, 2000), 51.
7. The other six instances are given in note 5 of Chapter Three.
8. S. Covey, *First Things First* (New York: Simon & Schuster,
   1994), 88–89.

Chapter Fourteen: Peter

1. W. Wiersbe, *Your Next Miracle* (Grand Rapids, Mich.: Baker Book House, 2001), 27.

Chapter Fifteen: Paul

1. (http://www.Psychneuro.Tulane.edu/Assesspert.html)
2. C. L. Rogers Jr. and C. L. Rogers III, *The New Linguistic and Exegetical Key to the Greek New Testament* (Grand Rapids, Mich.: Zondervan, 1998), 402.
3. Rogers and Rogers (1998), 304.
4. E. Deen, *All the Bible's Men of Hope* (New York: Doubleday, 1974), 201.

The Authors

Frank Minirth is president of the Minirth Clinic in Richardson, Texas. He has authored or coauthored more than sixty books, including the best-sellers *Happiness Is a Choice, Love Is a Choice, How to Beat Burnout,* and *Love Hunger.* He holds degrees from Arkansas State University, Arkansas School of Medicine, Christian Bible College, and Dallas Theological Seminary, where he is an adjunct professor.

He serves as a consultant for the Minirth Christian Group at Green Oaks Behavioral Healthcare Services in Dallas and at the Minirth Christian Services at Millwood Hospital in Arlington, Texas. For more information, please call (888) 646-4784 or go to www.minirthclinic.com.

Don Hawkins serves as the president of Southeastern Bible College in Birmingham, Alabama (www.sebc.edu). Formerly, he served as cohost and producer of the *Back to the Bible* radio program, which is on more than six hundred stations worldwide. He presently hosts the live nationwide call-in program *Life Perspectives.* A pastor for almost twenty years, Don is a graduate of Southeastern Bible College and holds graduate degrees from Dallas Theological Seminary and Calvary Theological Seminary. He has authored or coauthored over twenty books, including *Never Give Up, The Root of Inner Peace,* and *How to Beat Burnout.*

Roy Vogel is a psychologist and board-certified psychopharmacologist based in New Jersey. He is founder of Advent Counseling Centers and host of the New Jersey radio program *Lyrics to Live By*. Dr. Vogel and Dr. Minirth have broadcast over seven hundred short-form feature radio programs together.

Other Books of Interest

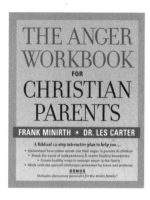

The Anger Workbook for Christian Parents

Drs. Les Carter and Frank Minirth

Paperback

ISBN: 0–7879–6903–6

"Parents will recognize themselves in this book. 'That's me, been there, and said that.' In easily implemented steps, the authors provide insightful, practical suggestions for changing the anger factor in family interactions."

—Dr. Garry L. Landreth,
Regents professor and director,
Center for Play Therapy, University of North Texas

"Les Carter and Frank Minirth give you all you need to know about how to use this dicey emotion to your advantage so that you become the parent you want to be. As a parent of two boys, I found this resource invaluable and I know you will too."
—Les Parrott, Ph.D., author, *High-Maintenance Relationships*

In this practical book, anger experts Drs. Les Carter and Frank Minirth—coauthors of the best-selling *The Anger Workbook*—show families how the "blame game" (parents blame the kids and kids blame the parents) doesn't work. Instead they provide insight for dealing with the root causes of anger. In a perfect blend of biblical wisdom and psychological research, they show readers how to understand what can be right about anger, distinguish between healthy and unhealthy anger, recognize how anger can be managed more successfully by controlling desires and insecurities and addressing other underlying issues, and much more. Filled with real-life examples, checklists, evaluation tools, and study questions, this valuable resource for any parent with a preteen or teenager will help parents understand and manage their children's anger—as well as their own—and show how to create harmony at home.